LOVE & DEATH

THE COMPLETE WORKS OF FORREST CHURCH

Author

Father and Son: A Personal Biography of Senator Frank Church of Idaho

The Devil & Dr. Church: A Guide to Hell for Atheists and True Believers

Entertaining Angels: A Guide to Heaven for Atheists and True Believers

The Seven Deadly Virtues: A Guide to Purgatory for Atheists and True Believers

Everyday Miracles: Stories from Life

A Chosen Faith: An Introduction to Unitarian Universalism (with John A. Buehrens)

God and Other Famous Liberals: Recapturing Bible, Flag, and Family from the Far Right

Life Lines: Holding On (and Letting Go)

Lifecraft: The Art of Meaning in the Everyday

The American Creed: A Biography of the Declaration of Independence

Bringing God Home: A Spiritual Guidebook for the Journey of Your Life

Freedom from Fear: Finding the Courage to Love, Act, and Be

So Help Me God: The Founding Fathers and the First Great Battle over Church and State

Love & Death: My Journey through the Valley of the Shadow

Editor

Continuities and Discontinuities in Church History (with Timothy George)

The Essential Tillich

The Macmillan Book of Earliest Christian Prayers (with Terrence J. Mulry)

The Macmillan Book of Earliest Christian Hymns (with Terrence J. Mulry)

The Macmillan Book of Earliest Christian Meditations (with Terrence J. Mulry)

One Prayer at a Time (with Terrence J. Mulry)

Without Apology: Collected Meditations on Liberal Religion, by A. Powell Davies

The Jefferson Bible

Restoring Faith: America's Religious Leaders Answer Terror with Hope

The Separation of Church and State: Writings on a Fundamental Freedom by America's Founders

Love & Death

My Journey through the Valley of the Shadow

Forrest Church

Beacon Press
Boston

Beacon Press
25 Beacon Street
Boston, Massachusetts 02108-2892
www.beacon.org

Beacon Press books
are published under the auspices of
the Unitarian Universalist Association of Congregations.

11 10 09 08   8 7 6 5 4 3 2 1

This book is printed on acid-free paper that meets the uncoated paper
ANSI/NISO specifications for permanence as revised in 1992.

Text design and composition by Yvonne Tsang
at Wilsted & Taylor Publishing Services

Library of Congress Cataloging-in-Publication Data

Church, F. Forrester.
  Love & death : my journey through the valley of the shadow / Forrest Church.
    p. cm.
  ISBN-13: 978-0-8070-7293-6 (hardcover : alk. paper)
  ISBN-10: 0-8070-7293-1 (hardcover : alk. paper) 1. Spirituality—Unitarian
Universalist churches. 2. Christian life—Unitarian Universalist authors. 3. Death—
Religious aspects—Unitarian Universalist churches. 4. Church, F. Forrester. I. Title.
II. Title: Love and death.

  BX9855.C48 2008
  289.1092—dc22
  [B]   2008013067

For Carolyn

Contents

Introit

Although I have delivered some thousand sermons on almost as many discrete topics, one way or another each circles back to a single theme. This tendency, I'm told, is not uncommon. Every minister worth his or her salt has at least one great sermon in them. It's no wonder we return as often as we do to its familiar music and uplifting chords.

Even church administrators pick up on their bosses' penchant to repeat themselves. In certain instances, they have little choice. Doubtless to restore his soul, one of my storied colleagues, James Madison Barr, of Memphis, Tennessee, had a habit of disappearing periodically, especially on Mondays and Tuesdays, when the office staff was composing and printing the weekly church newsletter. At the top of each newsletter, they included the sermon title for the following Sunday and a brief précis of its theme. Whenever Dr. Barr was missing in action and necessity forced the Memphis church administrator to be creative, she listed his forthcoming sermon as follows:

"The Great Mystery"
James Madison Barr, Preaching
What Dr. Barr will be preaching about this Sunday
is a mystery, but we're certain it will be great.

Great or no, my recurring sermon, too, is rich with mystery. Time and again, I return to the abiding theme of love and death. I have preached on this theme more times than I can number, almost from the outset of my ministry until today, some thirty years later. I have woven its essence into countless memorial services, including my father's funeral and the service we held the day after 9/11, and unpacked it in several books. Variations on the theme of love and death sound from my heartstrings.

Death is central to my definition of religion. Religion is our human response to the dual reality of being alive and having to die. We are not the animal with advanced language or tools as much as we are the religious animal. Knowing that we must die, we question what life means. The answers we arrive at may not be religious answers, but the questions death forces us to ask are, at heart, religious questions: Where did I come from? Who am I? Where am I going? What is life's purpose? What does this all signify?

Death is not life's goal, only life's terminus. The goal is to live in such a way that our lives will prove worth dying for. This is where love comes into the picture. The one thing that can't be taken from us, even by death, is the love we give away before we go.

Today, I turn to the dual theme of love and death with a new sense of urgency. On February 4, 2008, I informed the members and friends of All Souls Unitarian Church in New York City, whose destiny and mine have been linked for so many years, that my esophageal cancer, first diagnosed and treated in the fall of 2006, had returned with a vengeance and that my time remaining was likely to be numbered in months, not years. "I won't predict how my body will hold up during the course of treatment," I wrote, "but I can tell you what I hope to do. Though all of our stories end in the middle, with ongoing business piled high, I should like to end my story, if I may, by summing up my thoughts on love and death in a book that might bring as much comfort to others as you have brought to me. In it, I shall share what I have learned from you during the three decades I have been privileged to serve as your minister. Time and again, at your loved ones' deathbeds and together in my study, we have struggled to wrench meaning from loss, seeking to find our way through the valley of the shadow. Rarely acknowledging to yourselves (or even sensing) your great courage and remarkable insight, on occasions such as these you have taught me the lessons of a lifetime."

You are now holding that promised book, at once a summation of my life's recurring theme and my personal journey down the road of love and death.

My journey began sweetly, me curled up in my bed listening to my grandmother gently remind me, if I should die before I woke, to give the Lord my soul. I doubt that it will end that sweetly. But the comfort lingers. As your guide here—and mine, too, for I embark on this quest to test my heart's wisdom—I shall lead you through my life's most significant passages: my best friend's death when we were both nineteen; my father's death, six years into my ministry; and my parishioners' deathbeds, where I so often experienced love's triumph. I shall explore the ways in which love and death charged my books and sermons with meaning; my millennial breakthrough in kicking the bottle and rediscovering God; the impact of 9/11 on my life and ministry; my dress rehearsal for death, when cancer first struck; and the shifting sands I stand on now in the months leading up to my final reckoning. My valedictory sermons to my congregation encapsulate all I have learned about love and death and will serve as a fitting summation of my beliefs. I shall close with a theological coda, asking where God is when the boom falls; share my thoughts on life after death; and express my abiding belief in love after death.

Since my parishioners have taught me so much of what I've learned about love and death over the years, let me begin our journey by quoting one of them. On receiving the letter telling of my cancer's return, a longtime parishioner, who has known her full share of death, wrote me of her heartache. "My heart has been broken again," Camille wrote, "and for that I am overwhelmingly thankful; without love this would not be possible."

PART I

The Journey

A Life That Did Know Death

I didn't live with death as a child, but it was a constant visitor to my home. My earliest memory—doubtless fabricated from later stories, but real nonetheless—is of my mother, Bethine, nursing my father, Frank, through what everyone then thought was terminal cancer. I was a toddler at the time, so the image is surely one fragment of a patchwork quilt of collective memory that also found me lovingly passed back and forth between the arms of my parents' friends and those of my great-aunts during much of my early childhood.

We returned to Boise, Idaho, from Palo Alto, California, when I was two, my father in recovery and our tiny nuclear family tucked snug into a tiny house on Logan Street, where I popped tar bubbles in the driveway on hot summer days and roamed the neighborhood with my friends, playing Indians and cowboys. As the eldest of our little band, whether as a chief or cavalryman, I was killed in these mock battles less often than they were, but death was certainly the centerpiece of our play.

When I was five, my parents sold our house to help finance my father, Frank Church's, campaign for the U.S. Senate, and we moved in with my maternal grandparents. It was there that I witnessed my first death, that of my grandmother's father, Alexander Burnett, from emphysema at the age of ninety-five. Before he entered his death throes, my grandfather, Chase Clark, and I would visit him occasionally in his one-room cabin on the outskirts of Boise City. The two men would play pinochle as I took in the strange smells and sorted through the oddities of this laconic old man's house. As I remember, and my memory is as undependable as the Idaho weather, his three major food groups were tobacco, baked beans, and whiskey. The two men played in silence. He called me chatterbox.

During the final two months of his life, Alexander Burnett and his enormous oxygen tank moved into my grandparents' home, where he took up residence on the living room couch. Every day he grew weaker and, if at all possible, quieter, and then, one sunny afternoon, passed away surrounded by the family. The musty tang of his death is as vivid to me today as the smell of morning coffee. It was the most natural thing in the world.

Every Christmas, the entire, relatively small, Clark/Church family gathered at my grandparents' house for a week of festivities. Apart from a younger, crippled, cousin and her baby brothers, I was the only child for years, until my brother, Chase, joined the family when I turned nine. My little cousin, who suffered from a severe genetic case of muscular dystrophy, took over my great-grandfather's couch. She, too, we all knew, was dying, if in her own sweet time. One Christmas, her couch was empty. Death had paid another visit to our home.

I was raised as much by my grandmother as by my mother, who accompanied my father around the state for two years between the time I was five and seven as they ran together for the Senate. Jean Clark raised me attentively and well. She took me on Sundays to her Presbyterian church and tucked me into bed every night, where she taught me to say my prayers. "God bless Mommy. God bless Daddy. And you, Mom Mom, and Pop Pop," and—to postpone the inevitable—as many more blessings as I could tack to a single litany: Lala and Smoky. Chris. Jimmy. My guppies. The sun and the moon.

"That's enough, dear."

Like millions of other children, to close my prayer I would

then repeat words once passed down to her and to her parents before her: "If I should die before I wake, I pray the Lord my soul to take."

Gently my grandmother would smooth and kiss my forehead. "Sleep tight, dear. Don't let the bedbugs bite."

What a curious notion of comfort, to haunt children to sleep, interjecting specters of death and biting insects. I wasn't haunted, of course; I was lulled, in the spirit of that famous lullaby: "Rock-a-bye, baby, in the treetop, / When the wind blows, the cradle will rock. / When the bough breaks, the cradle will fall, / And down will come baby, cradle and all."

It's difficult to imagine a panel of modern childcare professionals stamping its seal of approval on this ancient verse or on the prayer my grandmother taught me, not to mention her playful goodnight warning. Yet, something deep is at work here. The coupling of night and sleep with death and danger is not accidental. These old-fashioned bedtime runes spring from a time when death and danger were embraced as so intrinsic to human experience that parents unselfconsciously prepared themselves and their children for them every sundown. In this respect, the words do carry a powerful implicit message. By definition, life is precarious. The most protective mother, cradling her child, sometimes cannot prevent the bough from breaking. No matter how hard they try, or how often they are reminded, sleeping children cannot keep bedbugs from biting. And when, like a thief in the night, death pays a visit, we cannot pray that the door be bolted or the window shuttered, only that the Lord may keep our soul.

Reflecting back on my grandmother and her simple faith, I sense that many of us today have lost something precious. Not dogma, not a rule book, but a sense of life that did know death, that accepted all-too-human as human enough, and led to a reconciliation of human being with human love, weakness, failure, and loss.

My grandmother was remarkably ordinary, by no means a

saint or a sage. She knew her share of suffering, but it was essential to her worldview. An upbringing in relative poverty. The loss of her first child. A near-fatal illness as a young woman, with a long convalescence. In many ways, her life was hard. Yet my grandmother appeared to have found something we all seek. She had made peace with life. She didn't demand more than life was likely to offer. I can't imagine her ever confusing wisdom with knowledge. As long as everyone in the family had more to eat than they wanted and the weather cooperated with her plans, she seemed fully content. When her plans were thwarted, she accepted that too. Deeply religious yet in no sense conspicuously pious, she never preached and rarely judged another, at least not openly. She took life as it came and died at the age of ninety-six.

I remember her nursing her father at home as he lay dying. I remember her knitting through the pain of her own acute arthritis and helping her drug-addicted sister make it from bed to table. I remember her teaching me to pray. What I don't remember is her ever complaining that life was unfair.

I admit I romanticize my grandmother. Though she lived until I was thirty-five, I never really knew her thoughts or fears. Accepting her lot as a caregiver, without ambitions beyond those assigned to most women of her time, she displayed a passivity that I may have confused with contentment. Given how strong she seemed and yet how quiet she was, I expect that she might have been a very different woman had she come of age today. Yet, my grandmother did appear to have understood one important thing about life that many of us resist acknowledging. She seems never to have questioned that life, by definition, is a struggle, with suffering its frequent cost and death its final price.

The Death of a Friend

From my late teenage years into my early twenties, I romanticized death. I would die young, I decided, dramatizing my otherwise innocuous life with a punctuation mark that would somehow wrest my felt passions into a memorable story. This certain knowledge added poignancy and an element of mock derring-do to my philosophic ramblings. I was drawn to heroes who died young: the American journalist John Reed, who died in Russia after covering the Russian Revolution; Keats, Shelley, and Byron, the great Romantic poets, whose phosphorescent lives and thoughts lit my adolescent imagination; and then Bobby Kennedy and Martin Luther King Jr., whose deaths tore the hearts from an entire generation of seekers. My imagination was vivid, but not vivid enough to envision a long life, running its course and fading with a sigh. For death to be momentous, it had to punctuate, dramatically and memorably, a young, vital life cut short in its prime. Perhaps a tragic death, which would require nothing more onerous than being struck down before I could hammer my life's promise into a modest fulfillment, was the only way I could think of to compete with my famous father, who rose to the United States Senate when he was thirty-two years old.

As sung and storied by nineteenth-century Romantic poets, death represents the consummation of the heart's unrequited longing. John Keats, though a young man, fell "half in love with easeful

Death." And so he sang his song to death, consecrated in the perfect voice of a nightingale:

> *Now more than ever seems it rich to die,*
> > *To cease upon the midnight with no pain,*
> > > *While thou art pouring forth thy soul abroad*
> > > > *In such an ecstasy!*

Having prepared the way so eloquently, Keats, in his death at the age of twenty-five, became a symbol for his fellow Romantics. Clearly he was at peace with death, more so than he was with life itself perhaps.

Nowhere is this Romantic obsession with death captured more tellingly than by Richard Wagner. In the "Liebestod" (Love-Death) from his opera *Tristan and Isolde,* Isolde expires in ecstasy on Tristan's corpse. Anticipating Freud, Wagner saw death not as the final frustration of desire, but as desire's fulfillment. Given that, short of death, our desires can never be fully satisfied, in the Romantic adolescent mythos death alone promises redemption—in Wagner's words, "the highest bliss . . . the bliss of quitting life, of being no more, of last redemption into that wondrous realm from which we stray the further when we strive to enter it by fiercest force." Interpreting his own text, Wagner asked (and answered), "Shall we call it death? Or is it not night's wonder world, whence —as the story says—an ivy and a vine sprang up in locked embrace o'er Tristan and Isolde's grave?"

Once we survive adolescence, to make peace with death is (for most of us) not to celebrate it as Keats or Wagner did, but rather to accept it as the fated end of every earthly journey, coupling such acceptance not to desire's fulfillment but to life's completion.

When I was young, I thought death took courage. I was wrong. Dying may take courage, but death requires little courage at all. It is love that requires courage, because the people we love most may die before we do. Dare to love and we instantly become vulnerable, a word that means "susceptible to being wounded." Our mother struggles for life in a hospital, or our son risks his in a distant land. At such moments the courage to love is nothing less than the courage to lose everything we hold most dear. Love another with all our heart and we place our hearts in jeopardy, one so great that the world as we know it can disappear between the time we pick up the telephone and when we put it down. Love is grief's advance party.

Every time we give our heart away, we risk having it dashed to pieces. Fear promises a safer path: refuse to give away your heart and it will never be broken. And it is true, armored hearts are invulnerable. We can eliminate a world of trouble from our lives simply by closing our hearts. Yet the trouble from which we are liberating ourselves is necessary trouble. We need it as we need breath. Since the most precious and enduring lifework is signed by love, to avoid the risk of love is to cower from life's only perfect promise.

We do not and cannot possess the ones we love, for we hold them on loan. This hard truth makes the courage to love also the courage to lose. It speaks most eloquently when everything we cherish is in jeopardy, when our expectations for the way life ought to be are interrupted and challenged by death.

Dalton Denton was my closest friend at Stanford. During the middle of our sophomore year he died of pneumonia while on a skiing vacation at Vail, Colorado. He had been out on the slopes just the day before. That morning he felt a little tired and somewhat congested, so he stayed in the cabin while his friends skied. When they returned home later in the afternoon, Dalton was dead.

Dalton was a blithe spirit, serious about life but not at all somber. He was tremendous fun to be with, and we spent almost all our free time together. He introduced me to scotch and

Beethoven, two habits he had picked up at Exeter. I suppose that he was the closest thing to a sophisticate I had ever encountered. We were dorm mates in our freshman year. Together we pursued —he successfully, I not—two striking girls, both actors, who were themselves best friends. More than once after an all-night conversation, Dalton and I saw in the dawn.

A week before he died, I told Dalton that I did not believe I would live past the age of twenty-five. This romantic, melodramatic flourish didn't impress my friend. He simply said, "Lighten up, Church. You've been reading too many existentialists. Besides, six years from now is a fantasy however you cut it. Today's the day. Don't ruin it."

He was right. And then he was dead.

For weeks, I could hardly function. Only after he was gone did I realize how much I loved him, how achingly I needed and missed him. I would walk down the street and hear people blathering on about nothing and go temporarily out of my mind. I remember once stopping and hitting a wall so hard that I almost broke my hand. With Dalton gone, life was both raw and without meaning. Only death seemed real.

Dalton's death was my first real moment of awakening. Initially, I awakened only to life's emptiness. As if to punish myself further for his death, I vowed to leave school, a notion quickly scotched by my father. But the emptiness remained.

What I know now about love and death, but didn't know then, might well have helped me negotiate my pain over Dalton's loss. Love and death are allies. When a loved one dies, the greater the pain, the greater love's proof. Such grief is a sacrament. Sacraments bring us together. The measure of our grief testifies to the power of our love.

Grief can be avoided. The logic is simple. Distance yourself from profound attachments. Attachments are risky. Lock the door of your affections. Board your windows. Armor yourself. Hunker down safe within your garden. Follow your bliss to some other level. Transcend the tyranny of the ephemeral, where pain, suffering, and grief attend our days. Even dream about death as the solution to life's pain. To the extent that these strategies work, they do so by parching the love from our hearts.

We can be crippled by grief, of course. There is such a thing as pathological suffering, which is any suffering that closes us off from others rather than connecting us to them. You can drown a soul with tears. This is not what I am talking about. I am talking about emptying ourselves that we may be filled, losing ourselves that we may be found, giving away our hearts even though they surely will be broken. And when they are, remembering that pain is a sign of healing, not only physical but spiritual pain as well.

Dalton's death was a turning point in my life. I had been playing games with death, relying on my own pathos to create a personal context for meaning. Dalton proved that death is far more real and love far more essential than I had imagined either to be.

He taught me something else as well, more important and abiding. We cannot protect love from death. But by giving away our hearts, we can protect our lives from the death of love.

৩ 3

Father and Son

My most intimate lesson of love and death came with the death of my father, almost a quarter century ago now. I learned that my father was seriously ill shortly before Christmas of 1983. He was losing weight and strength rapidly. We felt it might have something to do with a diabetic condition that was diagnosed shortly after he left the Senate. (Frank Church served Idaho in the U.S. Senate for twenty-four years, from 1957 to 1981.)

During the week before Christmas, my father went through a series of extensive but inconclusive tests. His condition was worsening, though the doctors could not determine the cause. When it became apparent that my father would not be able to travel, my first wife, Amy, and I immediately flew to Washington, where we found him weak but in good spirits. We returned to New York just in time for Christmas Eve and Christmas Day services at All Souls. It was to be the first of more than a dozen such trips over the next three months.

There were close to a thousand people at church on Christmas Eve. "To celebrate the birth of Jesus is to affirm life's sacred potential by attesting to the power of love to remake humankind," I told them. "With his birth we may each, in a way, be born again, renewed in that love which alone can save our world and give meaning to our lives." I was thinking of my father. I was thinking of a gift he had given me nearly thirty years before, *The Jefferson Bible,* and of Jefferson's own definition of religion: "It is in our lives and not in our words that our religion must be read."

I returned to Washington with my young son on Christmas Day and again with my daughter for New Year's Eve. My father was gaunt and jaundiced. I think that he knew he was dying. The immediate frustration, however, was in not knowing why. Shortly after New Year's we made arrangements for him to fly to Memorial Sloan-Kettering Cancer Center in New York for diagnostic tests and a surgical procedure to unblock his bile duct.

On January 12, they operated on my father, performing a bile-duct bypass procedure, only to discover an inoperable malignant tumor on the pancreas. The cancer had spread to his liver, and there was no hope for recovery.

Three days later I was scheduled to preach a sermon commemorating Martin Luther King's birthday. I spoke instead about my father.

જ

As many of you know, my father is seriously ill. In light of this, I know you will forgive me for changing my sermon topic and even for saying some things which you may have heard me say before. This morning, I need to grapple once again, in new ways and old, with love and death.

When I was two months old, my father was diagnosed as having terminal cancer. For over a year he had been having severe back pains, which he attributed to stress. He was newly married. He had just finished his first year at Harvard Law School, where he worked hard enough and did well enough to win early appointment to the *Law Review.* Ever since returning from China, where he served as an army intelligence officer during the Second World War, he had been in a great hurry to finish his schooling and establish a career. Back pain seemed to come with the territory.

You may remember the winter of 1948. It was a severe winter, with several great blizzards back-to-back. My mother is a very strong-willed woman. After one winter in Boston, she was not about to suffer another, especially with a baby on the way. And so it was that my father sacrificed his newly won position on the *Law Review,* and my parents packed themselves off to the more gentle and familiar climes of Palo Alto, California, where my father enrolled for his second year of law school at Stanford.

I was born in September. Throughout the fall, my father's back pains grew worse, leading him to consult a series of specialists at the Stanford Medical Center. The diagnosis was cancer. They immediately operated but the cancer had spread, and he was given no more than six months to live.

Had my father remained in the East he probably would have died that winter. As it happened, the Stanford Medical Center was sponsoring a radical new experimental program in radiation therapy for terminal cancer patients. Every morning he was radiated with a megadose of cobalt. He attended all his classes, studied through the afternoon, had dinner, and then got violently ill, fighting nausea until, exhausted, he fell asleep. This continued every day. At the end of six months, he weighed 125 pounds, but he was alive and the cancer was gone.

Just last spring, a friend gave me a book written by a woman who has been living with cancer since the early 1970s. Her name is Natalie Davis Spingarn and her book is entitled *Hanging In There: Living Well on Borrowed Time.*

In this book the author quotes from a letter written to her by my mother. "Bethine Church wrote to me recently that I am quite right in feeling that 'the cancer twilight zone is a world that other people haven't lived in.' Describing Senator Frank Church's fight with cancer thirty years ago, and their feeling that he then had only six months to live, she said that forever after he had been a different person. It had been somehow easier for him to do the things that needed to be done, and let the things that did not matter go. We are all different people during, and after, an experience with life-threatening illness."

I was reminded by this passage, and again during the past few days, of how much my parents have taught me. Most of it has been taught by example and not by words. They never sat me down to inculcate the lessons that both of them had learned when my father was so very ill. They simply incorporated those lessons into the way they live their lives. Ever since my father's illness and recovery, my parents have lived on borrowed time. Fully aware of life's fragility, they have not been afraid to risk and give of themselves fully. Life for them is not a given, but a gift. It is a gift with a price attached. That price is death.

Few of us are unafraid of death. Death is the ultimate mystery. But there is a way to counter this fear. It lies in our courage to love. Our courage to risk. Our courage to lose. Many people have said it in many different ways. The opposite of love is not hate. It is fear.

There are so many instances in our daily lives when our fears stand in the way of our potential to love. How many ways we find to armor and protect ourselves. We sense the risk, of course. That is the main reason we act in the ways we do. Every time we open ourselves up, every time we share ourselves with another, every time we commit ourselves to a cause or to a task that awaits our doing, we risk so very much. We risk disappointment. We risk failure. We risk being rebuffed or being embarrassed or being inadequate. And beyond these things, we risk the enormous pain of loss.

For instance, however much we try, we cannot fully protect our loved ones from fatal illness or accidental death. However much we love them, we cannot insulate them from failure and disappointment. However much we would wish to, there are times when we are powerless to heal or save.

We pay for love with pain, but love is worth the cost. If we try to protect ourselves from suffering, we shall manage only to subdue the very thing that makes our lives worth living. Though we can, by a refusal to love, protect ourselves from the risk of losing what or whom we love, the irony is, by refusing to love we will have nothing left that is really worth protecting.

We, of course, are ready with a thousand excuses. There is always a perfectly sound or prudent reason to refuse to come out of hiding, to budget our strength, to cover our flanks, to pretend that if we are careful enough we will not be hurt or look foolish or have to do something that we do not wish to do.

I am not talking here only about love between two people. I am also talking about the love of ideals and the love of institutions that embody those ideals. Whenever we ally ourselves with something greater than ourselves, we run risks, sometimes enormous risks. At the very least, such allegiances demand our time and our money and our energy. They call on us to come out of hiding. They call on us to risk our hearts by the giving of our love.

This morning we celebrate the birthday of a modern prophet and martyr, Martin Luther King Jr. His was a gospel of love, love answering hate, love overcoming fear and even death. He preached the kinship of all people, and witnessed to his faith by countering violence with nonviolence. Not unlike my father, he did not spend his life, he invested it in things that would ennoble and outlast him. His witness is a powerful beacon of hope that still illumines the public landscape in these difficult times. Certainly, Martin Luther King Jr. lived in such a way that his life proved to be worth dying for. Especially when it came to love, he knew that the only things which are truly ours are those things we are prepared to give away.

This, too, is the lesson that my parents taught me. I keep forgetting it, of course. It is one of those lessons that one has to learn over and over again. It is one of those lessons that we learn by doing and forget by not doing. It is the lesson of love. Love thy enemy. Love thy neighbor as thyself. Cast out thy fear with love. And then—this I know—it will be somehow easier for us to do the things that need to be done, and to let the things that do not matter go.

                                                                    ℘

Years before, my father had told me that his chosen way to die would be a massive heart attack. "One moment I would be walking down the street playing with a thought, the next moment I would be dead." What he feared most, and secretly expected, was a recurrence of cancer.

Fortunately, we are not in charge of our own destiny. After his senatorial defeat, my father was never quite at peace with himself. Yet, during the final months of his life he was able to make a closure that in certain tangible ways was redemptive. He was surprised by the outpouring of affection. He discovered that people held him in esteem not only in Idaho, but also in Washington and all across the country. For one whose only belief in immortality was to be cached in the bank of personal and historical memory, this knowledge was sustaining.

We, his family and friends, needed this time perhaps more than my father did. It gave us an opportunity again to say how much we loved him. And it provided us with one more chance to learn something important from him.

The decision to keep my father at home, without any life supports and in his own bed was, in our case, certainly the right decision. So often we die in unnatural surroundings. Most of us die in antiseptic environments, surrounded by strangers and attached to machines. Fortunately, more is being done within the medical community to humanize hospitals and to make it possible for more people to die with dignity. Even so, unlike in earlier centuries, our image of death is strongly colored by the feelings of estrangement and fear that so many of us feel when a loved one's life is invasively, if often impressively, fought for by people for whom death represents a failure and the prolongation of life, however diminished, a triumph.

Many of us, of course, would not be alive today were it not for the miracle of modern medicine and the devotion of its practitioners. It is simply that one casualty of the modern age is that most of us are distanced as never before from the experience of death. The most natural thing in the world has become a taboo.

My dad was typically wry on the subject. "Do you know why great men die well?" he asked me one day about two weeks before his death, answering his own question: "Because they have to."

At one level, this is certainly true. A public person does often have to die a public death. His or her public watches, if only from a distance, some seeking perhaps a strange form of voyeuristic satisfaction, others a glint of illumination to guide them on their own dark way. Daily the reporters would call our home. Visitors would be quizzed on "the senator's spirits," or "what he had for breakfast." For one who has played a role on the public stage all his or her life, death becomes a finale. Whether you have known and loved these people all your life, or know them only as interchangeable faces in the crowd, you don't want to let your public down.

Frank Church didn't. Until the day before he died, whenever there were visitors, he rose to the occasion. Finally, he could barely speak, but the last thing to go was his incandescent smile.

Before he lost his strength, my father would regale his visitors with stories. One he particularly enjoyed was the story of the old Indian chief who went into the mountains to die. His time had come. He ceremonially handed over his symbols of power and bade farewell to his family and friends. When all of the farewell festivities were completed, he took his bedroll and climbed to a favorite spot of his in the mountains. There the old chief fixed his bed, lay down, folded his hands across his chest, and prepared to be embraced by the Great Spirit to enter the happy hunting grounds. Finally he drifted off, only to be awakened some hours later by a drop of rain on his forehead. *Drip, drip, drip,* the insolent rain fell, until the chief was threatened by a veritable deluge. Not being able to stand it any longer, he cursed under his breath, picked up his blanket, and returned, tail between his legs, to his tribe, sheepishly announcing, "I'm back!"

I do not want to romanticize my father's death. It was hard. He was in considerable pain, and during the last three weeks of his life he became increasingly impatient with efforts to feed him or lift his spirits. He had no appetite. There were times when he resented being cajoled. About a week before he died, at a particularly dark moment, he said to my mother, "The worst thing about all this is that you can grow to hate the people you love the most."

From that point on, my mother, Bethine, stopped all attempts to feed him or to make him do anything he did not want to do. She told him that she was ready for him to go. She told him that she wanted what he then so profoundly wanted. She, too, wanted him to die. Mother asked my wife, brother, and me to give him our release also. He seemed grateful and relieved.

The last real conversation my father had was two days before he died, when cousin John Church came by to pay his last respects. "How are you doing, Frank—I mean, spiritually?" John asked. My father blinked open his eyes, looked at his cousin, and simply said, "John, it is very, very interesting."

About twenty of us in the immediate family, several old staff members, and a few close friends flew to Idaho for my father's funeral, which was held at the Methodist Cathedral of the Rockies. A note of celebration and thanksgiving rang clear. The tone was set by Thornton Wilder's words quoted on the program: "All that we can know about those we have loved and lost is that they would wish us to remember them with a more intensified realization of their reality. What is essential does not die but clarifies. The highest tribute to the dead is not grief but gratitude."

In my own remarks I said, "In a very real way, this celebration of my father's life is a family celebration. For you are family too. Dad thought of you that way. It is not just that so many of you care, as my father so deeply cared, about the quality of life, the preservation of our environment, the establishment of a just and compassionate society, the struggle for peace. Transcending each of these, this is a family celebration because my father had, and lived by, a profound sense of kinship of all people. We share the same home, this beautiful, fragile planet earth. We share the same fate. We are mysteriously given life, and for a brief time blessed with opportunities to love and serve and forgive one another as best we can. We are gifted with special powers for good, each of us is. My father devoted much of his life to helping us, individually and collectively, to realize and act upon these powers, not to settle for who we are, but to stretch and become who we might be. In so many wondrous ways, my father taught us how to live.

"He also taught us how to die," I said in closing. "In his life, my father was a bit like the daystar, rising early to prominence, brilliant in the dusk and against the darkness, showing other stars the way. When it came time for him to go, when his precious flame flickered, he was ready. Peacefully, naturally, with serenity and grace, he returned his light unto the eternal horizon. Like the daystar, my father went out with the dawn."

4

My Teachers

I didn't become a minister in any meaningful sense until I conducted my first funeral. Of all the things I am called on to do, none is more important, and none has proved of greater value to me, than the call to be with people at times of loss. When asked at a gathering of colleagues what gives most meaning to my work, I replied that, above all else, it is the constant reminder of death. Death awakens me to life's preciousness and also its fragility.

Many of the same guides who teach us how to live teach us also how to die. They many even do both at once. As her therapist told the writer Anne Lamott just before Lamott's best friend died, "Watch her carefully right now, because she's teaching you how to live." Lamott reflects, "To live as if we are dying gives us a chance to experience some real presence. Time is so full for people who are dying in a conscious way, full in the way that life is for children. They spend big round hours. So instead of staring miserably at the computer screen trying to will my way into having a breakthrough I say to myself, 'Okay, hmmmm, let's see. Dying tomorrow. What should I do today?' "

My father taught me as he lay dying. So have many of the parishioners who have enhanced my understanding of life by sharing their deaths with me. In this regard, ministers are particularly graced. People teach us how to die, and therefore how to live, almost every day. I have found that one can never have too many instructors in this regard.

After my first year at All Souls—arriving as a twenty-nine-year-old newly minted Ph.D., I was, if my memory serves, the youngest member of a relatively elderly congregation—the church president paid me a visit to assess my first year's work. "You've done a splendid job, Forrest, in almost every way. We only ask one thing of you. Could you please spend a little more time preparing your sermons?"

Ouch. I was doing those sermons by the numbers—twenty hours a week preparation, eight hours writing. Even if I had wanted to devote more time to composing them, I couldn't have found it, not if I wanted to perform my other duties as well. What I soon realized, however, was that time wasn't the issue here. Experience was. But experience, most significantly the experience of death and dying, was coming fast. In a congregation one-fifth the size All Souls is today, I performed thirty funerals in my first year (more than we perform during an average year now). Unwittingly, even unwillingly, my congregants were schooling me.

Late one evening early in my ministry, I received a call from the daughter of a parishioner who lived right next door to the church. Her mother, Jane, had died suddenly. She didn't know what to do. Could I come over and help? I leapt into my clothes and rushed over to find her daughter crying at the door and Jane dead in her bed. "What should I do?" Jane's distraught daughter asked me. Having never been called on to answer in this fashion to death's requirements, I didn't have the faintest idea what to do. So I followed my instincts (folding Forrest Church, the well-meaning but basically incompetent fellow mourner, into my suit pocket) and exercised my ministerial office. First, we will pray, I said. So we went to Jane's bed, joined hands, and held her cold hands in ours as I led us in prayer. For her immortal soul. For her daughter and grandchildren and friends. For a peaceful passage. And then the Twenty-third Psalm. Jane's daughter stopped crying and hugged me.

Next, I said, we'll brew a pot of coffee and I'll call the police and a funeral home. The police were necessary to declare the cause of death, and my friends at the funeral home would come and take Jane's body. Over the years, this practice became second nature to me. Before long, two no-nonsense cops had written up their report, then sat around the kitchen table with us and had a cup of coffee. The mortician arrived soon thereafter, quietly and gracefully wrapping Jane's body while her daughter chose a favorite outfit for her mother to be buried in. By the time they were done, other friends had arrived. We set a time for the funeral, and then, having fulfilled my duties, I kissed everyone goodbye, said a silent farewell prayer, and went home. Something happened to me on that fateful evening. I became a real minister.

From that day forward, I have walked with my parishioners and their loved ones into the valley of the shadow on at least a monthly basis over the past thirty years. Each journey is a privilege. I could tell you hundreds of moving stories. Here are three of them.

I

In the early 1990s, a long-standing member of All Souls took her own life. She suffered from inoperable liver cancer. When presented with her alternatives, she decided, first, not to try to prolong her life with drugs, and then, to choose her own time to leave.

I first met her—an elegant, confident woman—when her husband was stricken by cancer twelve years before. He wished to die at home. The doctors were not sure that was prudent. This particular couple didn't give a fig for prudence. I remember them lying on the bed together, going through old picture albums, watching the U.S. Open on television. He faded quickly, and then he died. Both of them were at peace.

This same woman went on to help organize the New York chapter of the Hemlock Society. Its meetings were held at our church. This made me a little uncomfortable. I believe in letting the fates choose the time for my return. But Lois assuaged at least some of my concerns. Her major issue was the cost to society of futile healthcare for the mortally ill. When she told me she was dying and of her plans—two wonderful trips, one to Wyoming, the other to Alaska—but also of her determination to choose the moment of her death, I could only admire her. She might have lived a few weeks longer, but she died well.

I had a long talk with her the day she died. I asked her if she was frightened.

"A little," she replied.

"It's such a mystery," I said. "Who knows what happens after we die?"

"I do," she answered. "I'm going to be part of the stars." Whether literally or metaphorically doesn't really matter. She is now part of the stars.

Three months before she died, this courageous woman wrote a valedictory poem. It closes with these words:

> *These days I take nothing for granted.*
> *Neither memories, nor the good smell of morning toast.*
> *Still nimble, my body follows all orders,*
> *And all five senses are acute.*

When did you last pause to offer thanks that your senses were acute?

II

"I'm just a regular guy," Michael told me the day he died. Perhaps he was worried that I might make too much of his courage in my eulogy. The Sunday before, Michael had to leave worship early. He was having a difficult time breathing. What he didn't know then is that a respiratory infection had settled in his chest, signaling the beginning of his final chapter.

Until his illness set in some three years before, Michael Beier had been a senior director of equity trading for a major bank in New York City. He loved his job, one filled with action and challenge. And he reveled in his family: his wife, Theresa; their little daughter, Carly; and baby Dustin on the way. On the treadmill at lunchtime one day, Michael's calf cramped up. After six months of tests—by an orthopedist, podiatrist, chiropractor, and three neurologists—Michael learned that he had ALS (amyotrophic lateral sclerosis), better known as Lou Gehrig's disease.

Michael soon began to dedicate this personal tragedy to the greater good. He became a vice president of the Muscular Dystrophy Association (MDA). Before long he was on the board of the famed Packard Center for ALS Research at Johns Hopkins. In 2001 he helped plan Wings of Hope, the MDA-sponsored reception that raised $320,000 for the center's research. The following year he chaired Wings over Wall Street, dubbed by one writer "the Night of 1,000 Traders," bringing almost $2 million to the cause. "At first," Michael said, "I didn't set out to be a Christopher Reeve type and get so involved in organizations. But then I decided I should do something now, while I could still speak."

ALS is a devastating condition. The negative-print image of Alzheimer's, which takes away an often otherwise-able-bodied person's mind, ALS traps a perfectly working mind in a disintegrating body. Michael was thirty-six when he learned he had it. The week he died, Michael and Theresa gave me a book they had home-published, beautifully bound and poignantly illustrated with family pictures, titled "I Love You Forever," by Daddy. Seizing this last chance to spell out his love clearly, Michael dictated the text during the last month of his life. It begins:

Dear Carly and Dustin,
This letter is so hard to write; it is one of the hardest things that I have ever done. Each time I try to dictate it, I become so choked up that I can't get the words out. It is so hard to think of everything I want to say. Since I've had ALS, I've done more thinking than I have in thirty-nine years. I've thought so much about doing this letter, but I

have never been ready to say goodbye to my beautiful kids. There is so much that I want to say, and that I want you to know. So, I'll do my best to tell you some of the things I have been thinking about.

Since Carly's most vivid and Dustin's only memory of their father will be of him with ALS, he tells them stories about how he and their mother met, their courtship and wedding, their favorite vacations, the children's birth. "Your mother is and has always been the number one priority to me," Michael tells Carly and Dustin. "I hope that you understand how wonderful our relationship has been. It wasn't because I had ALS or was sick. The ALS never affected our love. In fact, it was a test and we came out winning. Before and after I got sick, our love has been strong. The only thing that has kept us together is love."

Michael went on to compose a modern version of what in the Middle Ages was called an ethical will. In addition to a last will and testament distributing their property, medieval Jews occasionally passed on to their children a written bequest of their values. In sorting through my own family's papers, I came across such a will written by my great-great-grandfather, a Mormon bishop. Today, the AIDS epidemic in Africa is orphaning so many children that ethical wills are increasingly common. Often bound, as Michael's is, these books are filled with stories from the children's early childhood, which they otherwise might not remember, together with tips for living a good life, sealed by expressions of love.

Unlike in my great-great-grandfather's ethical will and those of many medieval rabbis, no warnings are attached to Michael's gift. Not "do this or else." No burden of guilt. As many parent-child relationships so sadly illustrate, love coupled with guilt forms an intrinsically unstable bond.

In "I Love You Forever," Michael shares his favorite food ("Chicken Parmesan with spaghetti"), color ("Right now it is blue"), and holiday ("Christmas because I love giving presents"). He tells his children about the movies and music he loves. And then he offers a few carefully selected and touchingly illustrated life lessons.

Take care of each other.
Walk away from trouble.
Use your time in school wisely.
Make sure you think before you speak.
Always ask for help.
Always eat the best part first.

He goes on to teach his children things he has learned about reading and money and friendship. About ALS and sickness and hard decisions. And about his growing faith in God. He also speaks to Carly and Dustin openly about death, assuring them that he is not afraid. He said the same thing to me the final time we met. Michael was not afraid of death, because he had made his peace with life.

A proportional relationship exists between the fear of death and the fear of life. The fear of death diminishes our trust in life by increasing our awareness of the risk of living. Diminished trust and an increased awareness of risk are two primary sources of fear's debilitating power. Having mastered fear, nearing his hour of death, Michael was able to open his heart fully. Many of us struggle to do the same, even years before our appointed time. Until we can embrace death as (along with birth) one of the two essential hinges on which life turns, we remain, at least to a degree, in hiding. Doors locked and windows shuttered, we are unable to let in joy and fully experience love.

It would be difficult to be as conscientious a parent as Michael was during the short time allotted to him as a father. But everything we really need to know is right there in the title of his book.

By calling it "I Love You Forever," Michael imparted the greatest of all truths, and therefore the greatest of all gifts, to his children: the wisdom that love, and only love, never dies. "I will always feel your love for me," he says in closing. "Always feel my love for you. With all my heart, Daddy."

The first public attention to ALS came in New York's Yankee Stadium, when Lou Gehrig announced to his fans that he had contracted ALS—a disease that was destined to be named after him. "Today I consider myself the luckiest man on the face of the earth," he said. "I might have had a tough break, but I have an awful lot to live for." Shortly before his own death, Gehrig reported with elation word of a new antidote that seemed to be working to arrest the rate of muscular degeneration. "I've got good news for you," he reported to his old friend Bob Considine. "Looks like the boys in the labs might have come up with a real breakthrough. They've got some new serum that they've tried on ten of us who have the same problem. And, you know something? It seems to be working on nine out of the ten. How about that?" Talking with him further, Considine discovered that Gehrig was the one for whom the serum had no effect. "It didn't work on me," Gehrig admitted. "But how about that for an average?—nine out of ten! Isn't that great."

I thought of Gehrig's words when I joined Michael and some twenty family members in his living room the morning of his final day on earth. He was in complete control of the situation. Giving us our marching orders for his funeral. Making sure that we were all taking care of one another. And asking for the last rites, which I, as a Unitarian, performed imperfectly. That was just the way he wanted it, Michael said.

Michael's funeral was a celebration. After watching a brief video highlighting his life, the entire congregation stood in applause. The truth is, Michael was just a regular guy. That's what makes his courage so inspirational.

III

I knew only this about the young couple who were driving me to the airport. Just before Thanksgiving, they had lost their eight-week-old daughter. No one knows why she stopped breathing.

Their minister told me the story. When he arrived at the emergency room, the baby was barely alive, having been revived and placed on a respirator. The doctors held out no hope. As minister and father stood helplessly by, the child's mother sang lullabies. Sweetly and softly, she sang her favorite hymns. "For the Beauty of the Earth." "Transience." "Morning Has Broken." My colleague, the late Irving Murray, who had served in the ministry for nearly fifty years, said he'd never seen anything like it. The following day, she requested that these same hymns be sung at her daughter's funeral.

As this couple and I traveled together toward the airport exchanging pleasantries, I tried to summon forth the courage to acknowledge their loss. This shouldn't have been difficult. I do it all the time. Yet, for some reason—perhaps rationalizing that they weren't my parishioners and therefore not my "responsibility"—I couldn't muster the necessary presumption to shift our conversation away from the weather and the morning news. But then Cathy and Stewart asked me about my family. "Do you have children?"

"Yes, I do."

"How old?"

I couldn't go on. Just as I was about to tell them how sorry I was about their baby's death, Stewart said matter-of-factly, "You should know that we lost our daughter this fall."

"I do know," I replied. "Irving told me. Nothing is more tragic than the death of a child."

Cathy commented crisply from the backseat, "Sometimes I get the feeling that other people have a harder time dealing with it than we do. It's so real to us. We know what we've lost. But other people can't face it. They can't talk about it. They're frightened."

"They're frightened of us too," Stewart added, "as if we had some kind of disease that they might catch if they got too close."

"You're absolutely right," I said, all too knowingly. "The only taboo left, the only subject almost no one dares to talk about in polite company, is not politics or sex or religion but death."

"We're doing pretty well," he continued. "Cathy's right about that, but we sure could use some help, and not just from the therapist we're going to. On any given day, one of us may need to work on the past, just as the other is trying to break free from it and focus on the present or make future plans. Yet with the whole world, our family and friends, tiptoeing around us, we are left almost wholly dependent upon each other. Sometimes the resources just aren't there."

"It's funny," Cathy added. "Though most people can't seem to handle talking about Sally's death and are awkward around us, when we are together with them, laughing or chatting about some silly thing, I get this odd feeling that we're being judged, as if our behavior were somehow inappropriate."

"Perhaps we should wear black and not speak to anybody," Stewart said and laughed. "That would take them off the hook."

We went on chatting, now easily. About the conspiracy of silence concerning death. About how the most natural thing in the world has been turned into a monster that people are frightened even to name. About Sally. About their decision to have another child.

Just before we reached the gate, I said, "You know, in God's eye, Sally's life is just as precious as your life or mine. Whether eight weeks in duration or eighty years, viewed in light of eternity the length of one life is indistinguishable from that of any other. What really matters is that she taught you something about how fragile life is, and how much we need one another. Even in her dying, Sally touched and changed her little corner of the universe."

"You may be right," Sally's father said to me softly.

"I know one thing," her mother added in a bright, clear voice. "Now, when someone I know loses a loved one, I'll be there with a casserole and all the time in the world."

5

Lifelines and Lifecraft

During the decade after my father's death, I began to gather my thoughts on love and loss, scattered throughout sermons delivered over the years, into books. Harper brought out a little trilogy on hell, heaven, and purgatory, in which I remythologized humanism, seeking more depth for my liberal theology. It was too abstract for my full liking, so I turned to a more direct approach, written in the language of pastoral theology, which had by then become second nature to me. In the mid-1990s, Beacon Press, with whom I had worked on an introduction to Unitarian Universalism (my denominational faith) and a new edition of *The Jefferson Bible,* published *Life Lines,* a book on suffering, with instructions for holding on and letting go, and, five years later, its sequel, *Lifecraft: The Art of Meaning in the Everyday.* Both books developed a theme that I found myself regularly interjecting into my pastoral counseling.

Let me try to draw you a picture of it. The glass we look through onto the world is like a lightly stained glass window. Each pane looks out onto some aspect of our life: our vocation and avocations, our spouse or companion if we have one, our parents, our children, our health. At any given time, some of these panes are likely to be rosy and translucent. We can see through them clearly and their tint casts a gentle glow on the prospect we look out on. My wife is happy. My children are doing well. My friends are there for me when I need them. I enjoy my job. And my hobbies invest my free time with meaning. Imagine, however, that one pane in the window that looks out over our life suddenly grows cloudy. What was translucent becomes first opaque and then almost impenetrable. The tendency is to press our nose up against that one frame, desperately trying to see through it. When we do this, we lose all sense of proportion. Our entire world goes black.

How easily this tendency can kick in when we are dying. The once clear pane of our health, which we rarely bothered admiring the view through when all was well with our bodies, goes dark, and we can see nothing beyond our sickness. With our nose pressed up against the one frame we can see nothing through, all our other lights go out. We then invest our life's remaining meaning in what may be impossible, namely beating our sickness. Nothing else matters.

There's nothing wrong with doing what we can to polish up this particular pane when it clouds over. Any number of things—modern medicine, meditation, alternative therapies—we can and should muster as cleaning supplies. What concerns me is this: Even as we do everything in our power to get healthy again, we may obsess so on our sickness that we lose appreciation for all those things in our life that we would dearly pray be returned to us if someone suddenly snatched them away. The loving-kindness of a spouse or partner. The care and concern of a parent or child. The joy of lifelong friends, whose friendship seems to blossom into full flower with the recognition that we may have precious little time to enjoy each other's company.

Near the end of this long chapter in my journey through the valley of the shadow, in my book *Freedom from Fear* (written after I had addressed my own fears more forthrightly by stopping drinking as the millennium turned), I came up with a mantra that has served me as well in sickness as it did before in health.

Want what you have.
Do what you can.
Be who you are.

Wanting what we have mutes the pangs of desire, which visits from an imaginary future to cast a shadow on the present, which is real. Doing what we can focuses our minds on what is possible, no more, no less, thereby filling each moment with conscious, practicable endeavor. And being who we are helps us reject the fool's gold of self-delusion. It also demands integrity—being straight with ourselves and one another.

Those who know my mantra sometimes test me with it. "So, Forrest, do you really want cancer?" "I want what I have," I reply. "To selectively eliminate all pain from our lives may work, for a brief time, for a drunkard or drug addict, but we cannot selectively wish away all that is wrong with us without including all that is right." Each day that I am sick, I pray for the sun to come up, for people to love me, for manageable tasks that I can still accomplish, for a little extra courage, for reality to blow all the detritus off my plate. In short, I back away from the bedarkened pane of my health to gain a prospect of the whole window I am blessed to look through. The light then dances again in my daughter, Nina's, eyes. I laugh once more at my little foibles. My son, Frank, and I celebrate the Mets' acquisition of an all-star pitcher. I call my dear friends, Jack Watson or Peter Fenn, on the phone and talk for an hour about everything under the sun.

Yes, I kvetch at unseemly waits at the chemo center (until I realize how many other folks have cancer and are waiting in line for their treatments also). I fall into a sour humor when my body wears down and cannot do what I want it to (until I shift gears and tackle something that lies well within my powers, like a moderately difficult sudoku or one of Robin Hobb's splendid fantasy novels, where almost every character is doing worse than I am). I even snap at my wife, Carolyn, when she tries too hard to fatten me up for the kill. But that, too, eventually is good for a laugh. So I do want what I have, even as I do what I can, which, right now, is hammering out this little book. Pray for the right things, and your prayers will be answered.

Here are five short meditations, drawn and adapted from *Life Lines* and *Lifecraft,* to help refocus the mind when failing health —our own health or that of a loved one—darkens the screen of our lives.

I

Life is difficult, fragile, painful, unpredictable, unfathomable, and limited. Simply put, everyone suffers. That is a given. Suffering is a birthright far more inalienable than happiness. And the shares are not allotted evenly. We need not look far to find evidence for this. How often innocents, especially children, seem to suffer an unequal, undeserved share of affliction. Since neither justice nor injustice is distributed proportionally, life is anything but fair. Not only does the rain fall but the sun also shines on both the just and the unjust. Just try to make sense of it. "I have seen everything that is done under the sun," the Preacher in Ecclesiastes writes, "and behold, all is vanity and a striving after wind."

Yet all is not hopeless. Despite our ignorance and suffering, hope emerges in the lifelines that connect us. The Preacher begins by finding meaning in our common fate. "The right happiness for men and women is to eat and drink and be content with all the work we have to do under the sun, during the few days God has given us to live, since this is the lot assigned to all of us." He then turns to the ways in which we can serve one another. We should not hoard our bread but "cast it upon the waters." We should "give a portion to seven and also to eight." "Two are better than one," he says, ". . . for if they fall, the one will lift up his or her neighbor, but woe to those who are alone when they fall, for they have no one to help them up."

We cannot avoid adversity, loss, or failure, but we do have a choice of how we will respond. One person's response to illness might be to equate health with happiness. Never mind that she was not particularly happy all those years when she was healthy.

Now she knows the real value of health, having lost it. Another person might respond very differently. For the first time in her entire life she might live each day remaining to her fully, taking special pleasure in common things, savoring her time with loved ones, knowing it to be brief and therefore all the more precious.

Everyone suffers, but not everyone despairs. Despair is a consequence of suffering only when affliction cuts us off from others. It need not. The same suffering that leads one person to lose all hope can as easily promote empathy, a felt appreciation for other people's pain. Grief, failure, even death, can thus be sacraments. Not that suffering is valuable in and of itself. If one suffers alone, suffering is no elixir. A sacrament symbolizes communion, the act of bringing us together. Suffering brings us together when we discover the lifelines that connect our hearts.

II

People who claim that higher knowledge will free us from suffering are fooling themselves. So too are those who place their faith in a perfectly tuned and well-fortified body. Don't get me wrong. It makes good sense to take care of our bodies. But to do so to the point of obsession only invites another form of pride. I have a friend who has given up alcohol, cigarettes, coffee, eggs, meat, milk, and the sun. He eats oat bran for breakfast, takes megadoses of vitamins C and E, rides his Exercycle religiously, and never uses his microwave oven. He may not live any longer than his least prudent neighbor, but as his doctor told him, it will certainly seem longer!

Things are getting difficult for people who devote their lives to postponing death. Almost every day something new is added to the list of death-abetting substances and activities. The latest killer, believe it or not, is dreams. According to a recent study, dreaming can be bad for our health, because when we dream our heart rate jumps.

The hard truth is, we all die of something. Vegetarians die.

Joggers die. Even people with low cholesterol die, many before their time. One can do everything imaginable to play the right numbers, to change the variables in our human equation, and still life won't check.

No one would dare blame a two-year-old who fell to her death for playing recklessly in a third-story window, even though the cause and effect in such a case is clear. Yet, oddly enough, many people who fall victim to mortal illness try desperately to figure out what they did wrong, so they can blame themselves. If we shoot ourselves in the head, death is our own fault. But even though smoking increases the likelihood of cancer, when a person dies at sixty of esophageal cancer, as I likely shall, it's not only his fault, the tobacco company's fault, or the fault of society for condoning smoking. When we die, however we may have lived, the ultimate culprit is not sin or squalor. The culprit is life. Life draws death in its glorious train.

III

The Israel Museum in Jerusalem contains a collection of tiny ceramic cups. These were sacramental vessels. People cried into them.

Your mother has just died. Someone you love has cancer. Your spouse has left you. You are struggling at work. As likely, you have simply broken down. You burst into tears. So you pick up your tear cup, put it under your eye, and weep into it. When you are finished weeping, you cap it and put it away again. It is a way to save your tears.

Why save them? Because they are precious. It doesn't matter why you cried, your tears are still precious, for they show that you care. A full cup of tears is proof that you have felt deeply, suffered, and survived. Their value is ratified by this simple parable from Jewish lore. When his student complained that he was suffering and so deeply confused that he could no longer pray and study, Rabbi Mendel of Kotzk asked him, "What if God prefers your tears to your studying?"

If we knew better, we would cry far more often than we do. Life is difficult. Some people pretend that it is not, that we should be able to breeze through. Yet hardly a week passes in which most of us don't have something worth crying about.

Men seem to have a particularly hard time with this. We are taught not to cry. Tough it out. Don't let your feelings show, lest you be perceived as weak and soft. Yet, at times of loss, an acknowledgment of weakness and softness suggests a tender heart. If there is a single person who can't find something worth crying about, I would not like to meet him.

Many of us men have a hard time crying because we are afraid of our feelings. Every time we express ourselves emotionally, we lose some control. As the self-protected, fully armored husband in Wallace Stegner's novel *The Spectator Bird* says to his wife, "If we could peel off the callus, and wanted to, there would be, untouched by time, unwithered, vulnerable, afflicted and volatile and blind to consequence, a set of twitches as beyond control as an adolescent's erections." Yet, for those of us who become proficient at maintaining control, the results can be even more disastrous. We take our feelings and strangle them. Then we are nothing but closed, tight, frightened little people, pretending that we have grown up and hoping that no one will notice how deeply we really do care. At first it is an act, a hard act, but over time, as we get better at it, it may become less difficult, perhaps because we really do not care any longer. If we fail to practice caring, hurting, and crying, over time we may forget how.

On the surface, this has advantages. A callused heart remains invulnerable. The best way to protect ourselves from being wounded is to avoid love, or to love only in little ways so that when we are hurt we will only hurt in little ways. That was not the fashion among the ancient Hebrews. They were not afraid to cry. Their tears were sacraments of love, which flowed from a deep spring. The fuller one's tear cup, the more a person was esteemed.

Great-hearted people, it seems, cried far more readily than small-hearted people. Life touched them more deeply, not only the pain of it but also the joy. They wept into their cups of tears until they could truly say, "My cup runneth over."

IV

It is tempting to seek meaning not in what we have, but in what we desire. When we do this we practice wishful thinking. Of the enemies that frustrate our search for meaning, this is perhaps the most traitorous. It places fulfillment forever beyond our reach, in what we do not have, in what we cannot do, in who we shall never be. Such fulfillment lies at the top of an endless golden staircase. Somewhere high on his climb to nowhere stood J. Paul Getty, the multimillionaire. At the end of his life he cursed his wealth and said he would trade it all for one happy marriage.

The quest for happiness is fraught with such pitfalls. Public people lament their loss of a private life. Millions of unknowns dream of being famous. Beautiful people find reasons to regret their beauty; plain people, their plainness. One man chafes under marital vows. Another mourns the emotional barrenness of one-night stands. One woman, a homemaker, wishes that she were as confident and as successful as her neighbor, a businesswoman. And right next door the very object of her envy envies her the husband and children that she herself sacrificed for a professional career. Just where you think that the grass would surely be green, it may be dying.

I am no longer startled by this. What startles me still, though it no longer should, is precisely the opposite. Often, just where you'd think that the grass would be dying, it is green.

A woman is dying. She has been given a month to live. She and her children gather around the bed and talk about old times. They watch a movie together on television. They look at family pictures. Their hearts are filled with love. Adversity doesn't always bring out the best in people, but it can. That is because adversity, not always but sometimes, tends to strip away our illusions. It forces us to work within tightly drawn and well-defined limits. When we do, everything within those limits is heightened. Little things take on a much higher degree of importance. We count as blessings things that at other times we simply take for granted. As the seventeenth-century English theologian Jeremy Taylor said after losing all his earthly goods: "I am fallen into the hands of publicans and sequestrators, and they have taken all from me; what now? Let me look about me. They have left me the sun and moon, fire and water, a loving wife, and many friends to pity me and some to relieve me."

Meaning doesn't emerge from longing for what we lack, things we have lost or will likely never find. We should wish to think instead for things closer at hand, like the sun's kiss good morning when it breaks through the blinds to inaugurate another miracle, another day.

V

It takes courage to laugh, especially when the things we are struggling with are no laughing matter. The most healing aspect about the courage to laugh is that it keeps us from attaching additional strings to our troubles, no matter how serious they are. The journalist Linda Ellerbee memorably attests to laughter's healing power when she describes enduring the trial of a double mastectomy by calling laughter "the mother of courage."

Whether leavened by humor, lifted by contemplation, or lightened and expanded by neighborly concern, the moment we stop defining (and restricting) it on our own narrow terms, life opens up. Once we understand the secret to it all—that "it's not about me"—we no longer cast fear's shadow.

How liberating this is. Rising out of our self-pity, we shake off the temptation to whine, "Woe is me!" and "Why do these things always happen to me?" Rather than wondering why we don't have what she has and can't do what he does and can't be who they are, we take the opposite tack. We do what we can, want what we have, and embrace who we are.

☙ 6

Trapdoors

Life is a gift, not a given.
One day we will go to sleep and not wake up again.
The path of life is strewn with trapdoors.
Every day is a miracle.

My children helped teach me this lesson. One day we were almost killed crossing the street right in front of our apartment building. I was walking them to their last day in school. Three-quarters of the way across, with the light in our favor and all of us dutifully holding hands, a car burst out of nowhere, hurtling around the corner at breakneck speed, ricocheting off the curb and swerving into our path.

Missing us by inches, the car skidded, fishtailed back into control, and disappeared down the avenue. I could barely breathe, my heart beating like a pile driver. In stark contrast, my kids just laughed, romping blithely down the sidewalk, jumping from tree to tree as they always did, trying to touch the leaves.

Deeply shaken, I did the obvious thing. I got angry. Not at the driver, of course. She was long gone. I vented my anger at the children.

"Did you see that car? It could have killed us. It almost hit us. It really did. We might all have been killed." But neither of them had been doing anything wrong. They were holding my hands, walking with the signal. I had nothing to teach them.

Only this, perhaps. Our lives are beset with trapdoors. Whenever the ground seems most secure, something out there has its hand on the lever. A massive coronary, an embolism, a drunk driver, a vagrant cell multiplying with mortal vengeance secretly within our body until the tumors it spawns literally take our breath away. Superficially at least, cancer may offer a harder death, but not the same shock that besets anyone who must answer the phone to learn that a perfectly healthy loved one is suddenly gone. When a trapdoor springs, we haven't time for regrets or second chances. It just happens. Swoosh. No goodbyes.

I tried to teach my children about life's dangers. We all do. Look both ways. Wear white after dark. Don't take candy from strangers. We answer their questions and dearly wish they'd ask us more. But put a mad driver behind the wheel and our answers mean nothing.

Trapdoors have one saving grace. They add to our appreciation of life, even as they threaten to extinguish it. Later that very day, walking my children home from school, they looked different to me, more vulnerable and precious. As we talked about their last day in school and summer plans, I loved them desperately.

It reminded me of something I have to struggle to remember, even today. Life is not a given, but a wondrous gift. That gift comes with a price attached. One day something will steal it from us. That doesn't diminish our lives; it increases their value. Fragility and impermanence ensure life's preciousness. We can truly love only that which we know we must one day lose. It took a trapdoor trembling beneath my feet and a crazed woman casting the shadow of death across my family's path to awaken me once again to the wonder of life and the blessings of love.

My kids had the right idea. We had just escaped from a brush with death. Why didn't I think to jump and touch the leaves?

The trapdoors we traipse over in our daily wanderings are invisible until they spring. All the more reason to seize joy whenever and however we can.

Once I was a speaker on a cruise ship. I awakened early one morning and went out on deck. The salt air was brisk, the air a canopy of clouds. One other passenger was standing by the rail. "Lousy day," he sniffed.

And then a deckhand carrying a bucket and mop came down the stairway happily singing. At this, my fellow passenger took great offense. "What do you sing on a good day, a dirge?"

"A good day. Why, this is a good day," the sailor smiled in reply.

"You've got to be kidding. I paid a lot of good money for this and what do I get. I might as well have stayed home."

The deckhand replied with a twinkle in his eye, "Sir, there's many a blind man who would give his eyeteeth to look out on this day."

Every day we live is a miracle, rich with possibility, even when, right off camera, the boom is about to fall. When I turned fifty, five-sevenths of the biblically promised three score years and ten (that I have won at least a fair portion of), having just seen the blockbuster movie, I preached a sermon likening our voyage on earth to a trip on the *Titanic*. It, together with the sermon that follows in the next chapter, sums up my midjourney reflections on love and death.

ↄ

I hope you've seen the movie. It's a great movie. Great as in big, wide, and grand. Anyone who carps about the dialogue or acting is missing the point. Neither is particularly good. But neither is the dialogue and acting in most of our lives particularly good. The great thing about this movie is that it puts us smack in the middle of a magnificent ship, which then sinks, in a bone-shaking way.

If we have even the slightest amount of imagination, life is precisely like that. We board this great ship, a ship far more magnificent than any shaped by human hands; we sail into the deep; we romance on the lower deck or preen on the upper; we fall in love; things happen that test our mettle; we rise and fall to occasions; and then, at the end of the story, there is always an iceberg. Cancer, a heart attack, a wild drunken driver, and our ship goes down.

I really liked this movie. Everything from the chandeliers to the dead bodies floating in the water. It dazzled my imagination, all the more so because I knew how it would turn out.

I also know how my own life will turn out. When my ship hits an iceberg I will either drown or live long enough for my ship to hit another iceberg. It doesn't really matter if I am the captain of my own ship or if fate is. All that matters, in both steerage and the ballroom, is our dreams and our tears, with even these transcended in the mystery of a sunset or the passion of an embrace.

What I just said is actually not quite true. Rivets also matter. And bulkheads. And a competent helmsman.

The *Titanic* is a morality play, one not all that different from Noah's Flood or the fall from Eden. By definition, morality plays teach us to be careful. But if all we learn from morality plays is to be careful, or not to take chances, we will always be in the audience, never onstage. In other words, if life is a cruise, nine times out of ten it will not be an adventure.

Take today's cruises. Since the movie came out, cruise bookings are up. Counterintuitive, isn't it? As one travel agent said, "The wonderful opulence that people saw in the movie has a good many of them saying, 'Wow, that was a sharp-looking boat.'" Great. Two of my college friends were killed in a sharp-looking car. At the other extreme, however, when I read that "problems with cruise ships nowadays run more toward things like a galley fire, or the air-conditioning going out; and meanwhile, the passengers are up on deck getting a suntan," something tells me that problems such as these contribute very little either to our character or to the drama of our lives.

Religion shouldn't be a pacifier. Religion should awaken us, throw open a window, point to a trapdoor. The problem with a place like All Souls, so beautiful, so soothing, with angelic music and well-crafted sermons, is not all that different from the problem with the *Titanic*. If we forget how dangerous the waters are, spending our lives rearranging deck chairs to catch the sun, lulling ourselves to the gentle background of a soothing sound track, we set up our lives to do only one important thing: watch them pass before our drowning eyes.

Think for a moment about your life. That's what lies in the balance here. Think about your loves, which, of all the things that may live beyond you, are the only things that really matter.

How about your parents? Are your parents still alive? Have you forgiven them? Have you surprised them by a sudden burst of affection while you still can? Have you forgiven yourself for repeating their mistakes? Even if they are not alive? Go out to the prow of your ship late one night and wish upon their star. Even their falling star. Wish upon it before it disappears across the bow of your life.

And your children. If you are so blessed to have children, did you wake up this morning and say to yourself, "I am blessed"? What a gift you have given, what a gift you have received! Have you taken the time to remember how hard it was being children? How much you had to do to insulate yourself, to feel less pain, to smother fear? Do you remember? Please remember. Don't just work hard and pay your bills and go to movies and attend church and forget.

How about your brothers and sisters? Or your old forgotten friends? When did you last call your old best friend? How long has it been since you dropped everything to think back on that night twenty, thirty, forty years ago when he saved you from yourself, when she told you what to do, when they threw that party for you, when your old best friends let you know how deeply you were loved?

Remember, we are on this magnificent ship. It is going to sink. It always sinks. The menus don't matter. Nor do the size of our accommodations, not really, not finally. Neither does the speed our ship is going or the weather or the ports of call. All that matters is stored away safe in our memories, too safely sometimes, so safe that the passion and connection are forgotten, as we choose from the wine list or worry about the coming storm.

Not only this: but also the opportunity of an afternoon and evening we almost surely have in front of us matters—not to hide in, not to sleep through, but to savor and to share. As in one memorable scene from the movie *Titanic,* when young Jack Dawson finds himself temporarily elevated from fourth-class quarters to the first-class dining room. "Well, Mr. Dawson," one haughty matron asks, "where do you live?" "My address is the *Titanic,*" he replies. "I have everything I need here with me: the wind, the sun, the ocean, and the pleasure of your good company." On what was to be the eve of his death, this young man was not making too much of nothing. He was making at least something of everything.

As for us, if we had any sense, when we came to church, we would feel the pews beneath us trembling, even shaking. We would imagine the collision. We would sense the water leaking through the hull. Here in church we would hear our hearts beating and the hearts of those we love pumping blood—this is not nothing—blood coursing through our veins, keeping us alive, but only for a time: a time to love, a time to throw open the curtains we have drawn to decorate and camouflage our lives.

I admit, crossing on the *Titanic,* I wouldn't have enjoyed that first four days on the Atlantic if I only had been worrying that my ship might hit an iceberg. There is something to be said for routine, for semiconsciousness, even for hiding. That something is safety. It may be an illusion, but it can be a useful and successfully sustained illusion for a very long time.

So let me argue against myself. Let me confess how pleasant it is to go through days, even weeks, without thinking about death, our own death or the death of our loved ones. A master of rationalization, I know full well how functional it is to worry only about little things, little failures and successes, to be nettled only by little envies and grudges, and to indulge lots of little pleasures: watching a game; reading a good book; taking in a show. Even coming to church.

An overexamined life is not worth living. I know that. Some of you who come to me for counseling are so wrapped up in your own and your parents' underwear that I sometimes wonder if you will ever get out, if you will ever get naked. Just remember, you are not alone on the *Titanic*. We are all here together, on this extraordinary ship—different classes, yes, and not enough lifeboats—but when it comes to death there are never enough lifeboats. The ship is magnificent but one day it will sink. All hands will be lost.

This advice may return to haunt you, but I commend you to ignore life's dangers as readily as you protect yourselves from them. Even as an overexamined life is not worth living, an overplanned life lacks wonder and spontaneity. The harder we work to get things exactly right, the more cautious we become, the more careful not to fail. Risking nothing, we stand to gain little beyond the security of a battened-down existence. We miss the sea breeze and the ball. We will know little failure, or only little failures, but consider the cost. Any sure thing is almost sure to be so carefully packaged that when we unwrap it, the size of the box will turn out to be so many times larger then the size of the gift that we cannot help but be disappointed.

So if you are struggling with a relationship, out of touch with an old friend, unsure of whether to risk a new job, uncomfortably estranged from your father; if you are hiding to be safe, taking care not to be wrong, I suggest that you take a chance. Don't wait until you are sure. Don't wait until you have it right. Though waiting till we have it right works for some things—mostly little things—often our most important decisions and actions are so fraught with danger that we will never surely get them right. If we don't fire before we take perfect aim, we may never fire at all.

Life is filled with danger. That's just the way it is. Finally, the *Titanic* always hits the iceberg. Hence this simple, if imprudent, bit of advice: Before it does, pick up the phone. Pick up the gauntlet. Do whatever it takes. Take a few chances. Dare to live before you die.

ↄ

Attending Our Own Funerals

Sometimes we learn love's lessons when we might otherwise be least receptive to receiving them. Because my entire theology pivots on paradox, this doesn't surprise me in principle, but almost always it astounds me in fact. I learned one such lesson watching Princess Diana's funeral.

Whenever couples attend a wedding, they can't help but reflect on their own union, perhaps even silently reaffirming their wedding vows from the back of the church as the nuptial festivities unfold in the chancel. The same thing can happen at funerals. We hear a life summed up, often extolled, and wonder to ourselves what might the minister and our loved ones say of us once we are gone. We cry for ourselves at funerals, not only for our departed friends.

When Princess Diana died on August 31, 1997, I responded initially with scorn at the media circus surrounding the death of a pretty, privileged, and spoiled young woman. Her funeral, as funerals often will, led me to reconsider. Offering a somewhat different angle of vision on love and death is the sermon I wrote later that afternoon. "September Song," so-named to inaugurate our fall season at the church, is one of eight of my sermons and addresses that the editors of *Representative American Speeches* saw fit to reprint in their yearly anthology. Written at a time when I was struggling with issues of self-esteem and drinking far more than I should, I'm not sure where my thoughts about Diana left off and the truth about me sneaked in.

⌘

How strange that this year's September Song was composed by Elton John, "Candle in the Wind," written in honor of Marilyn Monroe, brilliantly and appropriately revised for the funeral of Lady Diana. How about Mother Teresa? What song would you choose for her funeral? "All You Need Is Love"? Maybe "Ave Maria"? They wouldn't even have to be rewritten.

I had a sermon for this morning that you obviously are not going to hear. September Song. Endings and beginnings. A nice, nonthreatening, impressionistic invitation to the next season of your life. But our September Song has changed and my sermon with it. The subject is the same but the song has changed. The new song was sung yesterday morning. My wife set her alarm for six thirty and almost missed it. I tried to sleep through, continuing, even wanting, to believe that nothing all that far out of the ordinary was happening.

Fortunately, I failed. She was right. I was wrong. This past week's events had finally sneaked up on me. With Mother Teresa's death I was overtaken. This is no time for business as usual. Certainly not a time for cynicism. It is a time for us to pay our respects to two people who, in remarkably different yet strangely similar ways, changed our lives—not just by being famous, but by investing fame with meaning, by touching our hearts.

Let me step back for a minute to share my thoughts about a preacher's job. I'm just beginning my twentieth year with you. This is about my six hundredth sermon. I draw from a strong faith tradition, which, if not orthodox, invites me to explore everything from the scriptures to ancient philosophy to current events. But the object is always the same. For me, religion is our human response to the dual reality of being alive and having to die. This week two deaths both cast a shadow and shone a light on what it means to be alive and then to die. For several days I tried to avoid the shadow; yesterday I felt the light.

Let me tell you what I dislike about much organized religion. It obliterates the ragged edges of our lives, imposing in their place a sterile, dogmatic form that encompasses everyone and no one at the same time. Let me give you an example. Last Sunday, the royal family worshipped at their local church in Scotland. These two bereft boys, William and Harry, sat through a church service in which their mother's name and death were never mentioned. The preacher delivered a sermon he had written the week before Princess Diana died. It was filled with sly humor and correct theology. It had nothing to do with anything that really mattered.

Most weeks I can preach to you a sermon I have settled on a month before. At their best, such sermons are worth pondering. This morning I am simply going to give you my own, unpolished thoughts about what you are already pondering, the deaths and lives of these two women, so very different save in this: each was thrust into a caste system—Windsor and Brahman—and refused to be governed by it. Instead they let their humanity shine through by embracing the constituency of the rejected.

How many of you watched some part of Diana's funeral yesterday? You and about a billion others. I believe that we are one, all of us, mysteriously born and fated to die, but how often do we even get close to experiencing that? Yesterday we did.

So let me try to make some sense of this, for me as well as for you. I have to begin with a confession. I didn't want to preach about Princess Diana this morning. I decided on Friday, before Mother Teresa died; but until yesterday I was still ambivalent. I don't believe in fairy princesses. I didn't want to concede more to the death of a fashion plate than to that of a forgotten young woman in East Harlem, who surely died this week and left two children and whose name we shall never know.

The first thing that touched me was my wife's tears. They fell every morning and evening this week. Let me tell you something: don't try arguing with tears. They come from someplace deep. They almost always matter.

And then I too started to cry. I finally got it. Yesterday morning, the little envelope on Diana's casket that said "Mummy." And then the song. And Prime Minister Tony Blair reading First Corinthians 13 as it has almost never been read before, and then Lord Spencer, who spoke the truth, his love expressed in anger, and I was crying. Again and again.

As Lord Spencer said, Princess Diana was not a saint. Mother Teresa was. Yet, when I heard that Mother Teresa had died, I felt nothing other than respect and appreciation for her life. Let me put this bluntly: I didn't feel my own death. But when Diana was killed in a Paris tunnel, I did. Not that I wanted to think about it. I didn't. I fought all week not to. But I did. I felt my death.

Even that's not quite right. I felt death itself. Sudden, untimely, the trapdoor falls: bang, that's it. Remember John Lennon's last song: "Life is what happens to you when you are busy making other plans." Life, and especially death.

I read all the papers, all the pundits. I even half-agreed with most of what I read. But it wasn't until Lord Spencer spoke that I got it. Why did this woman touch so many hearts so deeply? No one had said this before. The reason she touched our hearts so deeply is that she felt unworthy. Isn't that amazing. She touched us because of her openly acknowledged sense of insecurity, because of her lifelong struggle with a feeling of unworthiness.

If you want to know what to do with your own sense of unworthiness, think for a moment about this woman. She touched the untouchables: first children with AIDS, then lepers, finally land-mine victims without limbs. Along the way she paid her price: bulimia, a desperate willingness to give love to anyone who would offer kindness in return. But just think for a moment about this unbelievably beautiful woman who had so little confidence in herself and yet somehow managed to give so much confidence to others.

That picture of her with Mother Teresa in the Bronx taken less than two months ago; we have all seen it. Mother Teresa didn't have—at least she didn't seem to have—a sense of unworthiness. But she embodied humility. Yet even here the two share something deep. As Princess Diana demonstrated time and again, humility is not always born from saintliness. It can also be born from a sense of unworthiness. In some ways, that is even more remarkable. A woman has everything anyone could want, everything other than love and self-esteem, which are perhaps the only things that we should really hope for in this life. And so what does she do? She gives her love to others and builds their self-esteem. In a zero-sum game, the result would be nothing. In life it means everything.

How strange it is that those we cannot help but keep remembering almost always die young. How even stranger that the only woman I can think of from the last century who already has anything close to the legendary status Princess Di will soon attain also struggled throughout her life with a sense of unworthiness. And how appropriate that Elton John honored both of them with the same song.

Marilyn Monroe didn't cuddle AIDS babies or fight for the abolition of land mines. But she possessed exactly the same magic Lady Di did. She was everyone's fantasy but her own. This was captured for both of them in Elton John's original song better than in Bernie Taupin's beautiful reworking of the lyrics. One line he changed could well have been kept: after Elton John sings "She lived her life like a candle in the wind," instead of "never fading with the sunset when the rain set in," leaving the words, "never knowing who to cling to when the rain set in."

What does this have to do with us? Surprisingly, though I fought it all week, almost everything. We admire other people's strength; but I think, when it comes right down to it, we identify with other people's weaknesses. We can identify with Princess Diana not because she was royal—none of us is—and not because she was beautiful—almost none of us is. When this beautiful person died, the beauty lost had nothing to do with her looks. In a strange way, as so often is the case with physically beautiful people, her looks in fact were as much a personal curse as a boon. Remember, this was a woman who often hated what she saw when she looked into a mirror. But when she looked into the mirror of other people's eyes she recognized their pain. It is this that opened our hearts to her and made her the people's princess.

A sense of unworthiness is not the same thing as humility. A person who feels unworthy may simply feel humiliated. This leads more often to self-absorption than to compassion. The distinction is important, because many of us feel unworthy when we measure ourselves against others, our parents' expectations, people more successful than we are in work or in love. But even as humiliated people are abased, humble people somehow manage to abound. That's the difference.

Princess Di's sense of unworthiness translated into something redemptive: a connection with others. Her death is tragic, not because her promise was unfulfilled, but because it was fulfilled and might continue to have been. Not her promise of happiness, the fairy-tale princess story we were invited to believe in sixteen years ago, but the larger promise of love given—if never, because of her sense of unworthiness, fully received. My guess is, this would not have changed. Yet, Princess Diana more than fulfilled her unwanted mission. She found a way to invest her pain in other people's hope.

Let me try to bring this home. Because of her position, her beauty, her grace, even her public vulnerability, this woman was bigger than life. Mother Teresa was also bigger than life. History only allots a saint or two every generation—public saints, at least. In my book, there are saints everywhere doing Mother Teresa's business. She was different only because of her fame, but rare therefore because fame does everything it can to destroy sainthood.

Yet, though both of these women were larger than life, Diana is the one to whom we can relate. And yesterday morning I finally got it. We relate to her because of her sense of unworthiness. That and her triumph, not over but in spite of it.

Earl Spencer said that his sister didn't need a royal title to "dispense her own form of magic." Neither did Mother Teresa, not even a title from the church. Neither do we. We don't need anything to dispense our own form of magic. We don't need to be titled, beautiful, or successful. We don't even have to have a sense of worthiness. All we have to do is help others: to see our tears in their eyes, to recognize that the same sun sets on each of our horizons, that the mortar of mortality binds us fast to one another, that we are one.

In a strange sense, we witnessed our own funeral yesterday. No, the pomp won't be there, the horses, the crowds; but when we do die the same questions will be wafting in the air. Did we take what God gave us and make the most of it? Did we overcome adversity when hard times came? Did we love our neighbor as ourselves? Perhaps especially this. And did we make the world a more loving and interesting place?

Elton John sang to Diana, and he was right: "You were the grace that placed itself where lives were torn apart." Could we be that? Could we be the grace that placed itself where lives were torn apart? I have to think so. We know about lives being torn apart. We have even done a little of the tearing. But so had she. And we are here. This is the day that we are given. A new year is beginning. It is our new year. So let us inaugurate it well. Let us give our hearts to others. Let us do this before, sooner than you might imagine, either they or we are taken from us.

∾

ও 8

Bringing God Home

Those who return at times of trouble to the Twenty-third Psalm as a lifeline know the central role God can play in comforting a grief-stricken life. In my journey through the valley of the shadow, God leads me by the heart. When God dwells in my heart, I abide in God's presence. I live in an apartment of the creation furnished by the Creator. However humble my abode, its occupant but animated dust, the whole universe is my dwelling place. God's dominion is my domicile.

It hasn't always been this way for me. For years I dealt with grief and fear less imaginatively: I drank. Shortly after Princess Diana's death and one year before the terrorist attacks, I put an end to my lifelong love affair with the bottle. Sobriety didn't change my theology, certainly not the premium it placed on the axis of love and death, but it did deepen it in one significant sense. I now fully felt what before I had mostly thought. My heart had always been in play—how could it not with love and death my abiding theme—but now a trunk line opened from my mind straight to my heart, a line that was almost always open. My longstanding belief in a distant God slowly transfigured itself into my felt experience of a loving God. Ah, what a world of difference: to feel, not merely know, what one believes!

During the final, most conflicted, decade of my drinking, I paid more lip service to God than I did devotion. My career continued to thrive. I didn't get drunk, I self-medicated. By outward appearances, my life prospered. But it was increasingly hollow at the core. Delving into this hollowness taught me (as I had heard somewhere once) that when we don't really believe in God, it is not that we believe in nothing; rather we believe in almost anything. Because my wife, Carolyn, refused to look the other way, and because I had grown bone weary of my penchant for evasion, I couldn't live like this much longer. All my excuses and rationalizations had far outrun their expiration date. After several aborted attempts and long experimentation with variously successful half measures, with the turning of the millennium in the year 2000 I quit drinking.

Taken literally (in Hebrew and Greek as well as Latin), *conversion* is not "rebirth" but "turning." Once converted, we redirect our journey. The American short-story writer Raymond Carver turned his life around by a decision to stop drinking. From that point forward, he met life's trials with equanimity and grace. When dying of brain cancer at the age of forty-nine, Carver summed up the nine years of freedom he had enjoyed during what turned out to be the final decade of his life with the same word that leapt to mind when I daily gave thanks for a yearlong reprieve from my cancer: *gravy.*

For every Raymond Carver, however, there is a Chris Antley, a convert who experiences the joy of redemption only to drift back to sea to be lost forever. Before dying of an overdose at the prime of his career, Antley was perhaps the greatest jockey of his generation. At the apex of his reign, he crowned at least one winner for sixty-four straight days. In 1999, scarcely a year before he died, Antley won both the Kentucky Derby and the Preakness, a feat all the more impressive because, to do this, he overcame an eating disorder that had ballooned his weight by thirty pounds.

Antley was brilliant, cocky, kind, and courageous. But he was something else as well. Chris Antley was powerless over drugs, food, and alcohol. He disappeared for weeks immediately following his wedding, an event he had called the happiest of his life. He returned to his wife, but in a deep depression. He couldn't shake drugs and appears to have run afoul of his dealers. Friends found him dead one day in the entryway of his home. They thought he had been beaten to death; toxicology results proved otherwise. Chris Antley was thirty-four years old.

After his first rehab, Antley told a friend about his newfound, hard-won faith in God. "God is in every one of us," he said then. "You just have to find him. Something was growing inside of me without my realizing how powerful it was. Before I was blind to see that. I had a paranoia about sharing my feelings. I was hiding behind a wall. I don't have to live that way anymore. I wish you could jump inside my body right now to know how good I feel."

Shortly before his death, Antley scrawled on his living room wall a drawing of a crucifix together with his anguished prayer: "Jesus Please Save Me." You could take this as proof that God does not exist and Jesus cannot save. In fact, it demonstrates only that competing gods hold their own destructive and captivating power.

Describing his four-month residence in a rehabilitation facility in 1997, Antley spoke of having "dug deep into the depths of my soul and faced down some monsters." The wonder is not that Chris Antley succumbed to the monsters he so valiantly strove to face down; it is that Raymond Carver and millions of others like him can look back from their deathbeds over their final years as a bonus, like pure gravy.

❦ 9

September 11 and the
Sacrament of Grief

In 2001, a national crisis reforged my theology of love and death in a crucible of anguish: the terrorist attack on 9/11. As a New York City minister, I couldn't help but take this tragic event deeply to heart. I focused my mourning in two ways: by raising a large fund for victims who might not qualify for immediate government aid, and by editing a volume of sermons delivered in houses of worship across the country and spanning the religious spectrum in response to this act of terror. George Gibson, publisher of Walker Books, brought out *Restoring Faith: America's Religious Leaders Answer Terror with Hope,* as an instant book, rushing it to bookstores by November 11. Neither of us took any profit, but we both benefited deeply from the experience. September 11 repointed my studies as well. I began searching for the essence of true American patriotism, a search that led me to write a biography of the Declaration of Independence (*The American Creed*) and two books on the founding fathers and matters of church and state (*The Separation of Church and State* and *So Help Me God*).

First on my agenda, and the nation's as well, was grief. All of us remember the sense of grief and horror that people across America felt immediately following the terrorist attack on 9/11. Over the next seven days, faith communities throughout the nation gathered to mourn the innocent and to seek guidance from their religious leaders. It soon became evident that an act of terror designed to tear America apart had instead, at least initially, brought people together. Nowhere was this more manifest than in houses of worship. In unprecedented numbers, people thronged to churches, synagogues, and mosques to grieve together and comfort one another. Tears were the sacrament of the hour.

I didn't hear of a single preacher who didn't scrap his or her planned sermon in answer to the emergency 9/11 call. Not since the weekend following President John F. Kennedy's assassination had any single event so focused religious proclamation in our land. In a sense, the entire country became a house of worship. The memorials that began on Tuesday, continuing on Friday in the National Cathedral, and then conducted in houses of worship all around the country the following weekend, were not (as funerals often are) services of closure. They were invocations of a long and challenging journey that the American people will be taking together for years to come.

Almost seven years have passed since that fateful day. With the American people now so passionately divided, I look back on 9/11 with one eye firmly fixed on what might have been. As subsequent events have made painfully clear, it is hard to fight a just, or proportional, war against terrorism. Our own misguided response has seeded the very jihad our leaders set out to quell.

At first, however, the terrorist attack brought us together as a people. In the days following the attack, people asked strangers in elevators if they were okay. Neighbors became extended family. And few of us failed to see our loved ones with new eyes. In my counseling, I talked to people who finally, after months, even years, of procrastination or rationalization, were ready to commit themselves to make something finer of their lives. "I've finally stopped drinking for good," one man told me. "I haven't been to church for twenty years," another confessed. "I've got to get my spiritual life in order." A third almost wept, "This has brought my husband and me back together. It's a miracle. I can't believe it.

We've lost three friends. A dear cousin. And yet somehow in the midst of this tragedy we found each other." The shadow of death brought them back to life again.

Foreshadowing at once a missed opportunity and continuing danger, here are the words I shared with my congregation on Tuesday, September 12, the day after the terrorist attack.

ev

How precious life is and how fragile. We know this as we rarely have before, deep within our bones we do. I am not certain how much more we know right now. Our minds imprinted with templates of horror, our hearts bereft with truly unimaginable loss, we face a newly uncertain future. The signposts have all been blown away.

I am so grateful to see you, each and every one. How profoundly we need one another, especially now, but more than just now. We are not human because we think. We are human because we care. All true meaning is shared meaning. The only thing that can never be taken from us is the love we give away.

So let me begin simply by saying "I love you." I love your tears and the depths from which they spring. I love how much you want to do something, anything, to make this all better. We all feel helpless right now; I know that. At times like these and today uniquely so, in the midst of our daily stroll through life, reality leaps out from behind the bushes and mugs us. How I ache for those of you who have lost dear friends and loved ones to this senseless and barbaric act of terror. How I ache for all of us, who awakened this morning to a new skyline, not only here in New York, but all across America.

The future as we know it is dead. Long after the smoke clears from lower Manhattan and the banks of the Potomac, our vision will be altered by the horror of September eleventh. No longer can we measure human accomplishment by technological mastery or by our standard of living. Henceforth, for years at least, we shall be remembered by two things above all others, one conveniently ignored, the other too often forgotten over decades devoted to material progress. Unmistakably and forever inoculated against innocence by this full-scale outbreak of terrorism's virus on our own shores, as a nation we shall be known by the steadiness of our resolve in leading the war against the perpetrators and sponsors of terrorism all around the globe. And as individuals, truly now members of one embattled body, we shall be known no longer by the symbols of abundance and prosperity. Hope will answer helplessness if, and only if, from the sacrament of this shared sacrifice of innocence and the innocent, we become channels for one another through which our faith may flow, and wells of love from which to draw much needed comfort and new strength.

At first these visions of a future rebuilt upon yesterday's ashes may seem to contradict one another. Justice and mercy. Anger and compassion. War and love. Yet they will only be at odds should we choose one vision in place of the other. On the one hand, if hatred and vengeance spur a lust for retribution, rather than the greater quest for peace, we will but add to the world's terror even as we seek to end it. On the other, if we pray only for peace, we shall surely abet the spread of terrorism.

History supports each of these statements. In the first instance, we must recall history's most ironic lesson: choose your enemies carefully, for you will become like them. Terrorism is powered by hatred. If we answer the hatred of others with hatred of our own, we and our enemies will soon be indistinguishable. It is hard, I know, to curb the passion for vengeance. When we see Palestinian children dancing in the street to celebrate the slaughter of our neighbors and loved ones, how can we help but feel a surge of disgust and anger, the very emotions that precipitate hatred. But the Palestinians are not our enemy. Nor are the Muslims. This is not, as some historians would have it, a war between civilizations. It is a war between civilization and anarchy, a war of God-demented nihilists against the very fabric of world order. I hope you will all go out of your way in the days ahead to practice the second great commandment and love your Arab neighbors as yourself. Few outside the circle of those who lost loved ones in yesterday's tragedy are more surely its victims than are the millions of innocent Muslims whose God's name has been taken so savagely in vain.

With the war to be fought one between civilization and anarchy, our only hope lies in the balance we strike as we enter this uncertain and forbidding future. It rests in how well we balance justice and mercy, retribution and compassion, the might of weapons and the power of love. Our hope hinges on how effectively we unite a riven world against an elusive foe. But it also requires that, singly and together, we answer the challenge of maturity that will arise so quickly from the ashes of our shattered innocence. To do this we must not only gird our minds; we must also prepare our hearts. Above all else, this is a spiritual challenge, one that each one of us must meet. If before we could seemingly afford the luxury of relegating our spiritual lives to the occasional Sunday, today, facing a transfigured future, we must redirect our energies and spirits. In times like these, measured against the preparation of our souls, all lesser priorities lose their urgency.

The Chinese ideogram for *crisis* juxtaposes two word-pictures: *danger* and *opportunity*. Even as our grief today can be measured by our love, the danger we now face suggests a commensurate opportunity. In the theater, a crisis is not something that happens, thenceforth driving the events of the play. In Greek the word *crisis* means decision. In the wake of this tragedy, it is the decisions we make that will shape our character and (to a degree) drive the plot our lives will follow.

If religion is our human response to being alive and having to die, the purpose of life is to live in such a way that our lives will prove worth dying for. Over the past two days, all of us have lived with a heightened sense of life's preciousness and fragility. We know how easily it could have been us right now for whom some dear one was about to light a candle. Yet the same thing that makes us more attentive to death can also bring us to life. This saving opportunity matches the danger we have witnessed and now feel. And we are just entering the period of crisis.

The survivors in this city, every one of us, have been changed by this tragedy and will continue to be changed by the decisions we make over the days and years ahead. We can decide to be angry, vengeful, hateful, becoming like our enemies and poisoning the one well. We can also decide that we can't do anything—that the world is hopeless—and go back to our trivial pursuits as if tomorrow were no different than the day before yesterday. Or we can rise to the challenge and pledge our hearts to a higher calling. We can answer to the better angels of our nature and join in a shared struggle, not only against our foes—who are the world's foes—but also on behalf of our friends and neighbors. We can listen more attentively for the voice of God within us than ever before. We can heed its urgings with acts of kindness and deeds of love.

This is already happening. It is happening here this evening. It has been happening on every street corner of this great and newly compassionate city, from sacraments of self-forgetting valor to the redemptive mingling of tears. Though our minds have been singed forever by imprints of horror, our hearts join in deep admiration for the ordinary courage and simple goodness of our neighbors, made one in shared suffering, reminding each other of how splendid we can truly be.

Never forget this. Never forget the e-mail sent by a doomed employee in the World Trade Center, who, just before his life was over, wrote the words, "Thank you for being such a great friend." Never forget the man and woman holding hands as they leapt together to their death. Pay close attention to these and every other note of almost unbearable poignancy as it rings amidst the cacophony. Pay attention and then commit them to the memory of your heart. For though the future as we knew it is no longer, we now know that the very worst of which human beings are capable can bring out the very best. From this day forward, it becomes our common mission to be mindful of both aspects of our nature: to counter the former while aspiring to the latter; to face the darkness and yet redeem the day.

℘

This memorial service marked but the beginning of a great city's mourning. Daily from September 18, 2001, until the end of December (and occasionally thereafter), the *New York Times* published brief obituaries of men and women who died on 9/11. We are used to reading obituaries of the famous and infamous. These were of ordinary people, their lives both as alike and as unique as fingerprints.

And what stood out in these brief obituaries? Not worldly success, nor a list of noted accomplishments and positions. In almost every instance, what stood out was love given and received.

> Scott M. McGovern
> Just before bedtime, Ms. McGovern said, her husband would pick up Alane, the older of their two daughters, wrap her in a blanket and walk out to the driveway of their house in Wyckoff, N.J. "Where are you going?" Ms. McGovern would ask them. Scott would whisper back, "We're going to wish on a star."

> Cora Hidalgo Holland
> "I loved my mother's hands, her extensions of her soul," Nate Holland, now 19, said in eulogizing his mother... "She had hands like silken clay, forever soft and always warm. When I was a child she would tuck me into bed and run them through my hair as we talked until I could talk no more. I would drift into sleep as her fingers floated

across my scalp. The second that she withdrew her hand I would awaken, her rhythmic lullaby ending, but I would still pretend to be asleep."

David S. Berry
"It was raining stunningly hard, and all the kids, of course, were running around the house naked," Mrs. Berry said. "David was running with them. Water was just coming down in buckets, and they remembered how it was coming down the gutter, like a faucet. In playing with the children there was no distraction," she said. "He was nowhere but right there in the moment, right there."

Christopher C. Amoroso
The other night, after Sophia Rose Amoroso had her bath, she looked at her tiny hands, wrinkled from the bathwater, and told her mother, Jaime, "I have Daddy's fingers." . . . She will [also] always have the letter he wrote her when she was 10 weeks old: "Sometimes it makes me cry, as I am overwhelmed by the joy I've been given by you and your mother. I want you to know that I consider myself the luckiest man to ever walk the face of this earth. If anything were to happen to me, I could honestly say I've known true love and happiness in my life."

Each of these brief notices is filled with heart—heart as gratitude and heart as courage. Love conquers fear because it cannot die. Michael Tucker's obituary closes with, "He was Michael, he was Mike, he was Tuck to his friends from school and he was Daddy, and he's still making us smile." In a memorial service for his two brothers, Keith and Scott, Todd Coleman said, "I will try to live my life in a manner that will be worthy of their respect and admiration . . . Their memory reminds me that the world can be a wonderful place." On the day he was to die, George E. Spencer left a note for his wife on their kitchen counter: "Stop being critical of yourself," it said. "Enjoy life. Today is another day. Chance to live a little."

Eternity is not a length of time; it is depth in time. We enter and meet there through the sacrament of love. Like Michael Beier's ethical will, the *Times* death notices offered ample testimony to the courage of people answering death's no with love's yes.

✑ 10

Love, Death, and Easter

If I were to come to church only once a year, I should choose Easter. Easter is a better choice than Christmas. Christmas doesn't have death in it, not at its very center anyway, and if you are going to go to church only once a year, church should have death in it.

Christmas does have animals and presents and babies and stars. These are all splendid things. And Christmas has birth. But Easter has death and rebirth. Birth is essential, but for our spiritual journey death and rebirth are far more consequential. Easter also has flowers, of course, but flowers don't really have anything to do with Easter. They have to do with spring. I have nothing against flowers. They are almost as splendid as animals, presents, babies, and stars. But Easter is not about flowers. Yes, flowers are beautiful for a brief season and then languish and die, just like we do. But then they cast their seeds to the wind, seeds which crack open, springing new life from the husk of death. It's a pretty metaphor. There is only one problem with it. We are not flowers. And Easter is about us.

I have no idea whether Jesus was physically resurrected or not, but I suspect he wasn't. If I am right, for many people that would be it for Jesus, period, end of story. Christianity would be a delusion, a miscommunication of events faithfully transmitted from generation to generation for two thousand years. File it with the Easter bunny under springtime fantasies. Bequeath it to Harvard psychologists as evidence of cognitive dissonance. Or to the Jesus

Seminar, a flock of New Testament scholars who, after thirty years of deliberation, can find no compelling evidence that the resurrection took place.

That this fails to shake my faith is irrelevant, because my faith isn't grounded in the bodily resurrection of Jesus. I ground my faith, my Christian faith, instead in the spiritual rebirth of Jesus's followers, a saving transformation as available to us today as it was to his disciples so very long ago.

Most Christians certify their faith by professing belief in the Apostles' Creed. Cast in its present form centuries after Jesus's lifetime, the Apostles' Creed posits saving power in four things: Jesus's birth from a virgin; resurrection; harrowing of hell; and heavenly investment on the right hand of God, whence he will judge the quick and the dead. It teaches that Jesus was born in a miraculous way and died in a miraculous way, not that he lived in a miraculous way, even as we, too, can live. This is not my credo. I do not believe with biblical literalists in the virgin birth and bodily resurrection of Jesus. Neither do I believe, as do some liberal Christians, simply in his teachings. Jesus's teachings are in many ways wonderful, but, as is true of all human teachings, they are also flawed, limited by cultural and personal experience. So where do I ground my Easter faith? Purely and simply in the saving gift of Jesus's love, transcending the power of death.

I am quite certain that Jesus suffered, thirsted, and felt forsaken in the anguish of his dying hours. I am equally certain that his followers were devastated when he died. They expected for him to live and save them. But then a miracle took place. Jesus did not live to save them. He died and saved them, which is all the more powerful, however you choose to interpret it. Jesus suffered, wept, forgave, and died. His followers failed, scattered, wept, found forgiveness, and lived, reborn of his death, children of his undying love. For him and for them, even after death, in his love Jesus lived on. In his disciples' hearts he reigned as never before. Everything that mattered about him was theirs now. The way he cast out fear with faith. His love of God and neighbor. His astonishing humility. His disdain for pretense and cant. His courage and his passion. Each was more present now than ever before because Jesus lived within them, not simply among them. That is the essence of the Easter experience. A transformation occurred. Jesus was reborn in the hearts of his followers. Death was the occasion, love the medium, and forgiveness the catalyst.

Since Easter is the quintessential holiday of love and death, let me close the first half of our journey together with an Easter sermon.

෴

For millions around the world, the greatest story ever told is that of Jesus the carpenter's son. Yet it is a story without any of the markings by which the world measures success. No riches. No earthly power. Not to mention that the hero dies young, branded a criminal and nailed to a cross. Yet, all of us, whether Christian or not, can draw meaning from his tale. His courage can sustain our courage and deepen our understanding of the complex interplay among love, death, and freedom.

Jesus entered Jerusalem with fanfare, leading a band of followers who believed that he was the Messiah. Within a week he was betrayed by one of his disciples, brought before Pilate, sentenced, and crucified. His followers disbanded and went into hiding, in fear for their own lives. His chief disciple, Peter, forswore him three times rather than admitting to any knowledge of him. This is not the way the story was supposed to turn out. By ancient tradition the promised Messiah, scion of David, king of the Jews, would march triumphantly into Jerusalem to be crowned. Apparently, this was the expectation of many of Jesus's Palm Sunday followers. The problem is, their expectations had nothing whatsoever to do with Jesus's gospel.

Reminding us that the world doesn't owe us a living—rather it is we who owe the world a living, our very own—Jesus's good news celebrates the gift of sacrificial love. Take his most challenging injunction. By loving our enemy, we give away our entitlement to revenge; we sacrifice our pride. We also sacrifice our sense of entitlement and all the pleasures that go with vengefulness, bitterness, and hate. Forgiveness, too, requires sacrifice. We must sacrifice self righteousness, our preoccupation with having been wronged, and the advantage of holding another in our debt. Finally, and most important, we must sacrifice our control over everything that lies beyond our power—including our control over others, over events, and over the future. Ultimately, the courage to be requires the courage to let go. Fear accompanies us all the way to the grave, but we needn't hold its hand or accept its cold comfort. The word *sacrifice* literally means "to render sacred."

When most believers reach out to Jesus, it is to the fully human Jesus. His are hands we can hold. When tears well in his eyes, we know our own are blessed. The fear of Jesus is just like our fear. He worries. He wonders if he has done all he could to accomplish his mission, and at the end of his life, for one dramatic moment, he fears that he has failed, that everything was for naught.

We know that Jesus struggled with fear as he hung dying on the cross. It is written all over his last words. Jesus almost never quoted Scripture, but here we find him, at the hour of his death, quoting not the comforting Twenty-third Psalm but the starker Twenty-second—not "I shall walk through the valley of the shadow of death and fear no evil for thou art with me" but "My God, my God, why hast thou forsaken me? Why art thou so far from helping me?" Instead of the comforting words that usher in the close of the Twenty-third Psalm, "My cup runneth over," Jesus moans, "I thirst."

Where, then, in this drama, is the breakthrough? Where does courage answer death? It comes first when Jesus further says, "Father, forgive them, for they know not what they do." He thinks not about his own fate but about the fate of others. He returns to the very essence of his gospel—to love our neighbor as ourself. And also to love God. Jesus completes his surrender of self by placing his life in God's hands, saying, "Father, I commend my life unto thy spirit."

When we feel that we are alone, that God is not with us— when our heart is filled with dread about life or about death—we can take to heart the saving fear of Jesus, his own sense of abandonment by God, his all-too-human thirst. We can reach out as he did, not only for help—though that is a very fine thing to do— but to help as well. Letting go, Jesus recalled his own saving truth: love your neighbor; love your enemy; God is love; and love casts out all fear.

Since Easter is the holiday of love and death, think about your parents for a moment. Since all our love is imperfect, honor their imperfect love. So much of what they felt or feel toward you and about you, you will never know. You will never know this unless and until, perchance, you too feel it in turn, perhaps toward children of your own, surmising then what your parents may have felt. Their amazement at your birth. The way they cradled you, helpless, wholly dependent, in their arms. Their unconditional love, however imperfectly expressed. How they sacrificed for you. You really never knew. You couldn't know. How they suffered when you burned with a fever as a baby. How much your pains in growing hurt them. How they wished they might suffer for you, protect you, make you safe from others and yourself, even from them, from all the inherited and acquired quirks and flaws that they brought to hearth and table. But they couldn't. And they probably knew they couldn't. They knew that nothing in their power, no amount of caring, even were they to do the impossible and get everything right, could protect you finally, either from life or from death. They also knew or know that you will never ever realize how deeply they loved you, not only because of their own failures as parents or people, but also because children, even grown children, cannot know these things, not really, not fully. Yet when they die, if they let you and you let them, their love, perfected of all blemish and confusion, lives on. It lives on in your heart.

Here, between parent and child, our most basic human bond, to consecrate death with love we must move beyond deciphering half-communications and miscommunications. We must move beyond reckoning all the ways in which our parents caused us pain by guarding themselves against it, even how much pain and fear they themselves endured without our knowledge in their poignant desire to protect and not to disappoint us. For this dance of love and death, forgiveness provides the music. To a lesser degree, the same is true of all our imperfect loves. We must move beyond reckoning to forgiveness, not only of others but of ourselves. Otherwise our love will remain captive, and when we die, it, too, will die.

Death is love's measure, not only because at a loved one's death our grief, however we express it, is equal to our love, but also because, when we ourselves die, the love we have given to others during our own brief span of days is the one thing death can't kill. Because we and our loved ones manage to devise so many ways for fear to bind our hearts—fear of intimacy, fear of disappointment, fear of embarrassment, fear of confrontation—because our fear of pain or possible pain manifests itself in so many guises, we often hurt each other without really meaning to. We hurt one another and ourselves by learning, over the practice of a lifetime, how to protect ourselves from pain. Add to this all the mistakes we make, and all the mistakes others make, and only one solvent can loose our hearts from self-protective captivity. Only love. And only a forgiving heart, one capable both of accepting and bestowing forgiveness, is open both to give and receive the saving power of love.

This is the essence of Jesus's gospel. We all are children of God. We all are sinners. We all can be forgiven if we will refrain from harsh judgment. Love casts out fear. God is love. And only love remains. Only the love we give away.

၏

The Destination

The Diagnosis

On October 17, 2006, I sent a letter to the members of my congregation to inform them that I'd been diagnosed with cancer. It read in part:

Dear Friends,

With apologies for sending this word out so impersonally, I'm writing to share with you the news that I have esophageal cancer. A bank of tests conducted over the past two weeks has confirmed the existence of a malignant tumor high in my esophagus, and we shall determine a protocol for treatment (radiation and chemotherapy or surgical removal) before the end of the month. Unhappily, this is a particularly fierce form of cancer; happily, it apparently has not spread. More important than any of these cold medical facts, I am in good spirits and more grateful than ever for the gifts of life and love. All four children have descended on the household, and Carolyn is girding herself for the struggle ahead. She'll be the general, I'm relieved to report; I'll simply be the battlefield.

After almost three decades as your minister, I have been graced with so many teachers, whose courage in face of life's troubles has been a constant inspiration. I can also happily report that the theology I have hammered out in your good company—religion as our human response to the dual reality of being alive and having to die, and the purpose of life being to live in such a way that our lives will prove worth dying for—offers the same comfort to me during my own time of trial that I pray it has given you in yours.

As for my mantra—want what you have, do what you can, and be who you are—I practice each every day, feeling myself blessed beyond measure. Please know that you live in my heart, an abiding presence that fills my life with strength and joy.

What appeared to be a death announcement had come by phone from my family physician, Dr. Marcel Laufer, at 12:30 PM on Friday, October 6. I had just returned home from a barium esophogram. The doctor began, "There's no way to dance around this, Forrest. You have what appears to be inoperable esophageal cancer." "How long do I have?" I asked. "Months," he guessed.

Carolyn was on the other phone. In fifteen minutes, a car was slated to pick her up for the airport. She was on her way to India to launch a major business project. My first challenge was not my health. It was somehow talking my willful wife into carrying on with her life. Even months, I reckoned quickly, is all the time in the world if you take it seriously and fill it with love. It was far harder for her to get on that plane than for me to insist she do so. We had plenty of time, I told her. Besides, I thought to myself, my life might be ending, but hers had to continue.

Until I had more information, I decided to tell only the All Souls ministerial staff and my three closest friends, one of whom lives in the city. My dear friend Robert Oxnam dropped what he was doing and arrived at my doorstep within the hour. Throughout my trials, he was a constant companion and abiding comfort. (I waited to tell the congregation until I had clearer news. By October 16, a CT scan had indicated that the tumor was operable and appeared to be contained in the esophagus.)

The next four days were much harder, I'm afraid, for Carolyn in India than they were for me in New York. For one thing, I had a sermon to write. For another, part of me welcomed the opportunity to absorb this sudden news on my own clock. Having spent my entire working life preparing for death's exam, I was curiously eager to sharpen my pencils and prepare for the coming test with as little attendant commotion as possible.

In retrospect, the most staggering thing about my reaction is that I cut straight to acceptance. I embraced the diagnosis at its grimmest and began girding myself to die. No disbelief. No anger. No bargaining. In fact, if anything, for a day or two I walked about in a pink cloud, feeling my death, getting used to it, finding my sea legs in what turned out to be remarkably gentle waters. Was my theology working? Or—I tested my equilibrium mercilessly—was I simply in denial or shock? With Robert, and later that weekend with Gary Dorrien of Union Theological Seminary, I probed to the felt edges of my experience to see if I could find a measure of pain appropriate to the sentence I had received. I was wistful, but never sad. What did overwhelm me was the simple finality of it all.

I couldn't wander too far into myself, for I had an immediate task at hand: the sermon. I changed my topic, as I always do when the world turns in a different direction than I had been intending to go, but this time without a pretext, since, among those present that Sunday, few besides Robert knew how my world had turned. I would preach a sermon entitled, "What I Believe." Nothing could be easier. For one thing, the barrel I had to draw from was overflowing. But the subject was also fitting. I wanted to test my beliefs, to see how well they met the exigencies of the hour.

Here, in part, is the sermon I preached on October 8, 2006.

છ

Religious experience springs from two primary sources, awe and humility. Neither awe nor humility is served by those who refuse to go beyond the letter—either of scripture or of science—to explore the spirit. Fundamentalists come in two basic varieties. Right-wing fundamentalists enshrine a tiny God on their altar. Fundamentalists of the left reject this tiny God, imagining that by so doing they have done something creative and important. Both groups are in thralldom to the same tiny God.

When people tell me proudly that they don't believe in God, I ask them to tell me a little about the God they don't believe in, for I probably don't believe in him either. *God* is not God's name. *God* is our name for that which is greater than all and yet present in each. Call it what you will: spirit, ground of being, being itself; it remains what it always has (in Rudolph Otto's definition of the Holy), a *mysterium tremens et fascinans*, an awe-inspiring, mind-bending mystery.

Theology is poetry, not science. During our brief span, we interpret the greatest and most mysterious masterpiece of them all, the creation itself. The creation is our book of revelation. We rely on the oracle of our own experience, drawn from our reading of the book of nature and of human nature, including our reading of the Bible and our study of philosophy. The text of meaning is vast, its nuances many and various.

In what I call the Cathedral of the World, there are scores of windows, each telling its own story of who we are, where we came from, where we are going, each illuminating life's meaning. In this respect we are many. But we are also one, for the one Light shines through every window. No individual, however spiritually gifted, can see this Light—Truth or God, call it what you will—directly. We cannot look God in the eye any more than we can stare at the sun without going blind. This should counsel humility and mutual respect for those whose reflections on ultimate meaning differ from our own.

Gaze into the light of the heavens. By latest reckoning (with 100 billion stars in each of 100 billion galaxies and 6.7 billion people alive on earth) there are approximately fifteen hundred stars for every living human being. The star-to-person ratio is fifteen hundred to one. That is awesome and it counsels humility. It should certainly discourage the scourge of human pride. But does it? No. Instead, we sit on this tiny, munificently fixtured rock arguing over who has the best insider information on the Creator and the creation. Is it the Christian? The Buddhist? The atheist? The humanist? The theist? Please! We human beings trumpet our differences, even kill each other over them, while, in every way that matters, we are far more alike than we are different. Theologically speaking, we are certainly more alike in our ignorance than we differ in our knowledge. In fact, by the time we die, we will barely have gotten our minds wet. The wisest among us will have but the faintest notion of what life was all about. This counsels humility, but it also affirms oneness. Truly we are one.

The acknowledgment of essential unity is the central pillar of my faith. In contrast, religious fundamentalists, rightly perceiving the Light shining through their own window, conclude that theirs is the only window through which it shines. They may even incite their followers to throw stones through other people's windows. Secular materialists make precisely the opposite mistake. Perceiving the bewildering variety of windows and worshippers, they conclude there is no Light. But the windows are not the Light; the windows are where the Light shines through.

To appreciate how enlightened this approach to religion is, consider this. If your neighbor disagrees with your personal theology, short of changing your mind—a prospect that may not delight you—you have only four options. You can convert, destroy, ignore, or respect her. Fundamentalists of the right usually attempt conversion, but sometimes, as we know firsthand from recent experience, they choose to destroy in God's name. Fundamentalists of the left tend to ignore such disagreements as irrelevant, but they, too, may choose destruction. One need witness only the gulags and crematoria to recognize that religious zealots alone have not cornered the market on muting the exercise of religious and political freedom by resorting to mass murder. In the

United States of America and as reflected in Unitarian Universalism, following the principle of *e pluribus unum,* we ideally embrace the fourth option: mutual respect. There is only one caveat to abridge such respect. We do not and must not permit stone throwing in the cathedral.

Why then do we choose to join together rather than exercise our full freedom to believe what we will in the privacy of our homes on Sunday mornings? Simply because experience has taught us that we need one another. We need guidance in recognizing our tears in each other's eyes. We need prompting to raise our moral sights. We need companions in the work of love and justice to enhance our neighborhoods and to strengthen our witness in the world. And, yes, we choose to join our hands and hearts because we know how easily we slip back into mechanical habits that blunt our consciousness. We need and know we need to be reminded week in and week out how precious life is and how fragile. So very fragile. And so phosphorescent. A year can seem to last forever, to the point that we may pray for it to end; yet decades flit past in an eyeblink.

Whenever a trapdoor swings or the roof caves in, don't ask "Why?" Why will get you nowhere. The only question worth asking is "Where do we go from here?" And part of the answer must be "together." Together we kneel. Together we walk, holding each another's hands, holding each another up. Together we do love's work and thereby we are saved.

Which leads me to this final thought. To be at home with life we must make our peace with death. Death is one of two hinges on which life turns; without death, life as we know it could not be. Each individual is the unique combination of gametes, not a copy replicated by division. For this reason, every time a woman gives birth, she gives death. Or to put it more gently, death is our birthright, perhaps life's only guarantee. At birth, we receive a life sentence that is also a death sentence. The particulars of each will differ, some aspects being mandatory (fated by the accidents of birth), others subject to parole for good, often courageous, behavior. Yet, immortality notwithstanding, though we may receive pardon and forgiveness during the course of our lifetime, the death sentence we receive at birth cannot be lifted.

To the extent that religion is a death-defying act, offering strategies whereby we can live forever, it may instead diminish our reverent appreciation for life, thereby representing a failure of awe. Remember, we were immortal once. We were immortal before we became interesting. Recalling our most ancient ancestors (single-celled organisms, replicated in each succeeding generation), at one time in the history of our evolution, death did not exist for us. Death came into the picture only when we evolved into sexual beings that reproduce their kind but not themselves.

It's not that I disbelieve in an afterlife; I simply have no experience of an afterlife and therefore have little to say concerning one. I do know this, however. First, nothing (including any imaginable afterlife) could possibly be any weirder or more amazing than life before death. Theology may begin at the tomb's door—the specter of death prompting reflection on what life means—but surely no revelation is more compelling or worth pondering than that of a newborn infant emerging from its mother's womb. When "doing theology," I try to remind myself that theologians are wise to close their learned tomes at times and reopen the book of nature. Theology's heartbeat is the miracle of our own existence. This miracle encompasses both birth and death.

To this miracle, we must each do everything in our human power to awaken. Awakening is like returning after a long journey and seeing the world—our loved ones, cherished possessions, and the tasks that are ours to perform—with new eyes. Think of little things. Reaching out for the touch of a loved one's hand. Shared laughter. A letter to a lost friend. An undistracted hour of silence, alone, together with our thoughts until there are no thoughts, only the pulse of life itself. Imagine an afternoon spent free from worry about the things we have to do, or an afternoon tackling tasks we have avoided. We may not understand any better than before who we are or why we are here. But for this fleeting moment—the one instant we can bank on—our life becomes a sacrament of praise.

If we follow Jesus's counsel and become again as little children, we may even dance in the ring of eternity. At the very least, by remembering that "Swing Low, Sweet Chariot" will play for us one last time and then the earthly strains will cease, we will join the dance of life with more exuberance. How much finer it will be, when our band is struck, if we have loved the music while it lasted and enjoyed the dance.

☙

I close worship every week with the same benediction. Perhaps I was only trying to ace the death test, but I uttered it that morning with more than my usual fervor, indeed with as deep a conviction as I'd ever felt in pronouncing it.

And now in our going may God bless and keep us,
May the light of God shine upon us and out from within us
And be gracious unto us and bring us peace.
For this is the day we are given.
Let us rejoice and be glad in it.

Bedside Manners

Within a month of my diagnosis, I awakened in the intensive care room at New York Presbyterian Hospital following successful surgery to remove my esophagus. Having never spent a day in my life in a hospital, I had to fight back my fears as I entered the unknown. As with so many of our fears, the reality of recovery proved less daunting than my dark fantasy had been. I woke up in the recovery room to be greeted by my wife and Galen Guengerich, my colleague and successor as senior minister of All Souls. From the outset of my illness, Carolyn has turned to Galen for pastoral counseling, and he has proved a wonderful strength to us both.

I didn't tarry in the hospital any longer than I absolutely had to. By marching around my floor thirty-six times the evening before my doctors gathered to make their decision on my dismissal, I escaped the hospital in seven days, the minimum projection for my stay. I marveled at the care I received. And I was buoyed by the uptick in my odds for survival.

I shall spare you the details of my recovery. Beyond my vanity in boasting surprising valor in meeting most of my trials, they don't signify much in the whole scope of things. I shall take this opportunity instead to offer a few tips for hospital visitors, the value of which became real to me during my weeklong stay. In the realm of sickbed etiquette, there are few available guideposts. Here are mine.

Apart from health professionals, I know of almost no one who doesn't find hospitals forbidding. In large part, this anxiety stems from fears concerning our own mortality. Everywhere we look we are faced with reminders of pain, sickness, and death, all the more haunting in the context of a hospital's imposing impersonality. Yet, someone we care about is ill. We are bringing ourselves as gifts. When we arrive at our friend's bedside, we must break through this veil of impersonality and our own protective armor to ensure that our discomfort doesn't prevent us from bringing aid.

We skirt our direly sick or dying friends for a second reason as well. We are mortified that we won't know what to say and, therefore, will make some fatal gaffe. Driven away by our fears, we absent ourselves from pain's table, just where our presence might be most welcome.

Let me try to defuse this problem for you. You don't really have to say much of anything. Just showing up speaks volumes. It takes but a very few words to console another—to be with her in her aloneness. "Can I get anything for you?" you ask. "Can I help you adjust your pillow?"

To comfort another—to bring him your strength—takes more practice, in large part because it requires you to be more comfortable within yourself. Break through the invisible barrier estranging you and your life from him and his illness, and you will be halfway there. Find little ways, anecdotes and stories, to assure him of your love. Extol your favorite ball teams. Recall the most significant passages of your friendship. Remind him of what he's taught you. Tell him that you will always be there for him. Bring him your strength.

Soon, before you know it, you will be commiserating. Commiseration is the deepest form of succor. All barriers broken down, your friend's misery will have tapped the source of your own and you will enter effortlessly into the language of empathy. Not "I know how you feel," because you don't ("I know how you feel" trivializes the patient's solitary journey), but "I can almost feel your heart beating in mine, you seem that close to me."

Because he is that close to you. With commiseration all false barriers between well and sick come crumbling down, and we are truly one. We cry together, laugh together, feel together whatever must be felt at such a sacred time. We experience communion.

There are several simpler, yet very useful, points of hospital etiquette. First, once you have greeted the person you are visiting, please sit down. Pull a chair beside her bed or perch on the edge of it. If you remain standing, it appears as if you're poised to leave. Besides, since you don't stand when visiting a friend in her living room, pay her a like courtesy here. Not only will this make your visit more relaxed, but you will be at eye level with your friend. All day long, people hover over her bed, looking down on her. Even if you are going to stay for no more than five minutes (often a good call, by the way) give her a break. Have a seat. Greet her eye to eye.

Second, be sure to touch her. In hospitals, touch is often invasive. It hurts. Touch is the probing of sensitive organs or the insertion of an IV. For this reason, nothing soothes like the loving touch of a friend. Smooth her brow, run your fingertips down her arm, hold her hand.

Third, don't tell her how good she looks, even if you are surprised to see her looking better than you had feared. This courtesy won't fool her, only make her feel less real and more self-conscious. In fact, don't come in planning to tell her much of anything at all. Let your friend set the tone and subjects of your conversation. Try question statements such as "It really must be difficult?" This will permit her to lead the discussion wherever she chooses.

Fourth, if your friend is seriously ill or in considerable discomfort, don't stay too long. Five to ten minutes, sitting down, holding hands, talking quietly, is just about right. The quickest way to wear out your welcome is by lingering to prove how much you care.

Finally, if she seems fated not to get better, don't tell her that you know everything will turn out fine, that she'll be her old self again in no time, up and dancing around. Such feel-good banter may make you feel better; fooling ourselves almost always does, at least for a spell. But, tragically, it may set her up for failure. When she doesn't get better, she will feel as if she were disappointing all those who have been cheering her on. The cruelest trick we can play on someone who's dying, unless she begs for it for reasons all her own (which must be respected), is brazenly to tell her that we know that she is not dying. Far better to hold her hand and tell her, whatever comes, that all will be well. Tell her how much you love her. Let her see you cry. Tears water the soul. Tell her that wherever she journeys, she will always be with you. In fact, apart from false bonhomie, there is almost nothing you can say that will make things worse, as long as your words are inflected by love.

I have one more gentle hint for you. Be kind to the nurses. For one thing, you may very well be in their way, and they have a job to do. But there is another, more important, reason. Your kindness to them will help remind them that what they are doing is more than a job; it is a ministry. All of us who have had good hospital stays have been blessed with good nurses. With their smiles and gentle touch, even when they are obliged to hurt us, they remind us that there are people in our bodies. Nurses are heroes. Thank them for caring so kindly for your loved one. It will break through the grim routine of their work and remind them of how truly special they are.

∾ 13

Unfinished Business

During my three-month convalescence, I kept in touch with my congregation by letter, the first of which I wrote a week after returning home from the hospital. "The surgeon has successfully removed the cancer from my esophagus by excising the offending organ and attaching my stomach to my neck," I wrote. "I now possess a promising, if not yet fully functional, 'estomagus.'" "Carolyn," I added, "has been brilliant throughout, permitting me to focus my full attention on the task at hand. Your loving thoughts, letters, and e-mails have been a magnificent boon to me. Committed to heart, they will continue to grace my life whatever the future may bring."

Being hooked up to a food pump for twelve hours a day was no picnic, but neither was it particularly onerous, and my days began to take on the appearance of normalcy. I still couldn't swallow, and, courtesy of a paralyzed vocal chord clamped during the operation, neither could I speak (I squeaked), but one can get used to almost anything. Besides, I was bathed in love.

"Feel and gather strength from the love and prayers that are radiating to you from the congregation," one parishioner wrote, and I certainly did. Another confessed, "Whenever I am faced with a crisis, I retreat to my Catholic roots and start lighting candles," sweetly adding that her first thought on hearing of my illness "was to run to the nearest church and deplete the wax supply on the Upper East Side."

Kindness is an underappreciated virtue. In fact, few if any

virtues are so pure. In the weeks following word of my illness, the members of my congregation sent me over a thousand letters—loving, compassionate, poignant, kind letters wishing me well. I walked through the valley of the shadow holding a thousand hands. Never have I felt more privileged.

Why is kindness so pure a virtue? Precisely because kindness is a gift that demands no response. For each such act of kindness, you get nothing tangible in return, save the feeling, the sacrament, of human sympathy. Kindness is by no means inferior to love. In fact it is a kind of love, agape, God's love, poured out upon the earth without a quid pro quo—a pure, unadulterated gift.

Do you remember *Love Story,* when Erich Segal writes, "Love is never having to say you're sorry"? Well, that's the stupidest thing I've ever heard. Love is having to say you're sorry over and over again, because love—eros, romantic or personal love—does demand a return on its investment. The kindness of agape is different. When I tell my parishioners I love them at the end of every sermon, I don't expect anything from them in return. When they took the time to write those notes and letters, they didn't demand anything of me. We were dancing in a circle of kindness.

By late January, I was getting my voice back and returned to the All Souls pulpit. This gave me several opportunities to unpack my newly won firsthand experience of battling with cancer. One of the first topics I tackled—still probing it to test any hint of denial at its core—was the way I cut straight to acceptance on first hearing what appeared at the time to be a death sentence. I came up with an explanation for my ease of mind that, to whatever extent it may be true, has practical consequence for how we might prepare for a death sentence years before it may be issued. The key is unfinished business. How much of it do we have left when the boom falls? The less unfinished business we have when it is time for us to go, the less regret we shall suffer for lost opportunities and the more attentively we can prepare our departure.

⌘

Some of you know from personal experience that a scrape with death makes our hearts beat, not only faster but also more insistently. Aware of life's limit and fragility, we truly mean it when we say, "This is the day we are given. Let us rejoice and be glad in it." Much of the time, almost inevitably, we drift through our days. Life lives us, the sand unwatched as it runs through our glass. Death threats are wake-up calls. No longer able to take life for granted, we seize the day and receive it as a gift. We unwrap the present and offer up a prayer of heartfelt thanks.

This doesn't always happen, of course. Elisabeth Kübler-Ross, before she got lost in the mystic haze, did important studies of how people respond to their own death announcements. Shock. Disbelief. Anger. Bargaining. And then—finally, yet only perhaps—acceptance. The lesson here is simple, yet profound. We cannot embrace our life fully until we find a way to accept our death.

This morning I wish to share with you a few insights I gleaned from my own passage through the valley of the shadow this fall, when I was diagnosed with cancer. First indications were that I had only months to live. For ten days, until more promising test results began to trickle in, I was on death row, dead man walking. During this two-week period, I learned something important, not just about myself but about freedom—something that has deepened my appreciation for life and also for death.

After my October 8 sermon, "What I Believe," when I returned home that Sunday afternoon to call Carolyn in India, it had become clear that I was prepared, or at least felt prepared, to go gentle into that good night. Accepting things we cannot change frees the spirit to attend to matters within our control. Rather than flailing, I felt a deep calm. My theology hadn't failed me. I was ready for the journey. My acceptance was strong, almost an embrace. And it sustained me throughout my illness, first through the valley of the shadow and then, when the campaign toward recovery began, on through my surgery as well.

Don't get me wrong. I wasn't happy about the prospect of dying. I had things left to do in my life and regretted the interruption of all my splendid plans. A book lay unfinished, in which I had invested great interest and hope. Not to mention my loved ones and the plans we, too, had for a future together. In short, I had scads of ongoing business that it now appeared I might be unable to complete. My acceptance, however, abided in a deeper place. I was free to die, I realized, because, although I had much ongoing business, I had no unfinished business. I had made peace with myself, with my fellows, and with God.

Never before had I made the connection between unfinished business and a dread of death. Yet, how often in my pastoral counseling had the subject arisen, when talking to survivors who had not been able to make peace with a loved one, often a parent, before he or she died, or listening sympathetically as they mulled over a life of missed chances and lost opportunities. In such cases, their unfinished business stood almost no chance now of completion. They would remain estranged or their dreams remain unrealized until the end of their days.

How often I have counseled dying congregants whose death sentence seemed to mark the bitter end of a long, unsuccessful struggle to make peace with themselves. The opportunity had passed, or so it seemed. At times like that, *if only* are the two saddest words in the English language. "If only I had done this or not done that." "If only I had wrenched myself free from some soul-destroying habit or had had the courage to act in some other life-restoring way when I still could." My task on such occasions was to remind them that their story was not over, not yet, that there still was time. And indeed, I've witnessed amazing last-minute reconciliations and conversions, truly courageous and successful two-minute drills at life's close that almost miraculously turned the defeat of death into a victory. But, in each of these cases, when acceptance came, it came hard. And often it didn't come. There was not world enough or time.

While my wife was in India, I mulled such things over in my mind. I tested the sturdiness of my acceptance and found it strong. Without really knowing it, I had, you see, taken care of business, in my case by stopping drinking some seven years before and then by following the spiritual disciplines attendant to faithful recovery. I had conducted a fearless moral inventory, made amends where it was possible and appropriate, recovered my good conscience, made peace with myself, with others, and with God. If I hadn't, when this apparent death sentence came, I know that I would have been crippled by regret. Never have I been so grateful to have attended to my unfinished business when I still could, while there was yet time.

I had more to learn, however. Smugness, which I was teetering on, is not, I quickly was reminded, a lofty spiritual perch, however pleased I may have been with myself. You see, my wife came home from India, stubbornly unprepared to bathe with me in the calm waters of acceptance. She quite appropriately reminded me, by her very presence and concern, that my death wasn't my own, to do with what I pleased. In short, I may have stumbled upon one of life's secrets, but it was not time to rest yet. I still had more vital work to accomplish.

Her principal concern, quite appropriately, was for the children. They, too, she reminded me, had their own unfinished business to attend to, business with me. Nathan, our youngest, took a leave from school, expressly because he wanted me to know the man he aspired to be, not just the boy he had been. Each of our four children, in his or her own way, needed to make closure with me on their own terms. They needed to say things they had not said. Show me things about themselves I had missed. Make a deeper connection with me that would sustain them after I was gone.

Little of this was about me. It was about them. Yet, clearly I had more changing to do, in order to be fully present to their needs. Mere acceptance, you see, was too easy, too selfish. The network of relationships, which binds us, and sometimes entangles us, with each other, has its own moral demands that we cannot meet on our own, only together. So I was confronted with a new batch of unfinished business to take care of. Much—not all, I'm sure, but much—of that business we, together, were able to attend to. It was difficult, bracing, humbling, yes, and sobering, but finally healing, a healing that touched from soul to soul.

What I'm talking about here, by the way, is salvation. The Latin root, *salve,* means "health." The Teutonic cognates *health, hale, whole,* and *holy* all share the same root. Being an agnostic about the afterlife, I look for salvation here—not to be saved from life, but to be saved by life, in life, for life.

Such salvation has three dimensions: integrity, or individual wholeness, comes when we make peace with ourselves; reconciliation, or shared wholeness, comes when we make peace with our neighbors, especially with our loved ones; redemption, in the largest sense, comes when we make peace with life and death, with being itself, with God.

All our lives end in the middle of the story. There is ongoing business left unfinished. We leave the stage before discovering how the story will turn out. In the meantime, however, to help ensure a good exit, one thing is fully within our power. We can take care of unfinished business. We can make peace with ourselves, reconcile, where possible, with our loved ones, and free ourselves to say yes to the cosmos, to embrace our lives and deaths, to make peace with God.

To be free to accept death is to be free, period. The courage we need comes before, when we face our own demons or reach out across a great divide to touch hands. It is life work not death work, but it pays great dividends down the line. So, if you need to, put down that drink. Or pick up the phone. Or take that long postponed trip. You know what your unfinished business is. Don't wait until it's too late to begin taking care of it. Death may come as a thief in the night, but it cannot steal from you the love you have given away, the strength you have shown in facing life's hardships, or the courage you have proved in quelling your inner demons. In taking care of your own unfinished business, and in helping your loved ones take care of theirs, you can liberate yourself and them from suffering that, if you wait too long, may one day become intractable, written in indelible ink, darkening the pages of your book of life.

Above all, by taking care of business you will improve the story you are in. Today's works of love and acts of conscience weave themselves into a plot that will continue long after you are gone, yet be changed for the better by your deeds when you were here. Life may not be immortal, but love is immortal. Its every gesture signs the air with honor. Its witness carries past the grave from heart to heart.

☙

It would be slightly unfair to urge you to attend to your unfinished business while you still can, without offering at least a few hints as to how you might accomplish that trick. We reform to live better lives, not to have better deaths, but the promise of a good death is certainly a bonus on down the line. So let me share with you ten simple hints on beginning—on how to reboot your life, if it has become dysfunctional or stale.

1) Begin here. How deeply you would long for all the things you take for granted, if suddenly you lost them. So much of what we want we have already, so want what you have.

2) Begin now. You have everything you need. Everything. Plus the bonus of today, one day more than you will have if you wait until tomorrow.

3) Begin as you are. At your fingertips is a treasure trove of memories and dreams. Put one good memory together with one good dream and you are ready to begin. (Good memories are

memories that make you feel good about yourself. Good dreams are the stuff of which tomorrow's good memories are made.)

4) Begin by doing what you can. No more, but also no less. Don't throw yourself against the wall. Walk around it. You can't do the impossible, but so much is possible. So many of the things you haven't tried you still can do. To get around the wall, you can set out in either direction—the wall has two ends. The important thing is to start walking.

5) Begin with those who are closest to you. They can cheer you on only if you let them. Invite them to give you a hand—bow. And to lend you a hand—ask. And to take your hand—no one can take your hand if you bury it in your pocket. You say they won't cheer you on, help you out, or take your hand? Maybe not, but how will you know without asking?

6) Begin by turning the page. Today you can open a new chapter of your life. If you are trapped in your story (stuck in place, botching the same old lines), revise the script. Practice a new line or two. When reading a book, we sometimes reach the bottom of a page only to realize we have been glossing its words without registering their meaning. We haven't been paying attention. We don't have the faintest idea what we've just read. So we go back to the top of the page and try to concentrate. It happens again. Sentences dissolve into words. Words into sounds. The books of our lives are no different. Resist the temptation to wallow over some dark passage until you know exactly what went wrong. You never will. Besides, perfection is not life's goal. Neither is unnecessary pain. If you are stuck, open a new chapter. Turn the page.

7) Begin by cleaning up your slate. Don't erase the past. File it by experience, to keep it handy should you need it. But don't obsess over it. Ticking off a growing list of grievances gets you nothing from life's store. As for the things on your "To Do" list that you'll probably never do, place them under a statute of limitations. Not only is there no reason to carry over your little failures

from one day to the next, but you'll also never reform the things you can about yourself until you stop trying to reform the things you can't.

8) Begin by looking for new questions, not old answers. Answers close doors. Questions open them. Answers lock us in place. Questions lead us on adventures. Socrates boasted himself the most ignorant man in Athens. Each new insight raised a dozen questions, extending the compass of his ignorance. Yet beyond every ridge he climbed there lay a wider vista. The more questions we have, the farther we can see.

9) Begin with little regard for where your path may lead. Destinations are overrated. And never what we imagine. Even should we somehow manage to get where we are heading, we won't end up there. Until life ends, no destination is final. In fact, the best destinations are those we look back upon as new beginnings. Good journeys always continue. So don't be driven by desire (that empty place within you), never to rest until you reach your goal. Invest your joy in the journey.

10) Begin in the middle. Our lives will end midstory, so why not begin there? Don't wait around for the perfect starting pistol. Or until you are ready. You may never be ready. No reason to wait in the grandstand for some official to guide you to the gate. Jump the fence. Enter the race in the middle. Begin here. Now. As you are. By doing what you can. With those who are closest to you. By turning the page. Cleaning up your slate. Looking for new questions, not old answers. And with little regard for where your path will lead.

Finally, before you begin, a bonus suggestion—begin small. Dream possible dreams. Set out to climb a single hill, not every mountain. Soul work needn't be strenuous to be high impact. You can begin transforming your life with a single phone call. Or by writing a kind letter. Or by opening your blinds to let the sun flood in. Don't say it's nothing. It's everything. For you have now begun.

Beating the Odds

By February 2007, it appeared as if I might have dodged the bullet. A CT scan showed no sign of the cancer anywhere in my body and my recuperation had gone so swimmingly that I was able to return to most of my regular duties. Covering my bets in case the cancer should return, I signed up with a new medical team at Memorial Sloan-Kettering Hospital, one of the world's premier cancer-treatment facilities. Throughout my medical journey, Carolyn and I have benefited greatly from the counsel and assistance of our dear friend Dr. Martee Hensley, an associate in women's oncology at Memorial. She introduced us to Dr. David Kelsen, a man every bit as kind as he is talented, under whose care I continue to this day. Dr. Kelsen isn't an odds maker, but he could tell me that if the cancer hadn't recurred within three years, I would likely be out of the woods. I certainly felt well. So I decided that I was healed.

If Dr. Kelsen was shy of making predictions, the Internet, as it had since the beginning of my illness, supplied all the fodder I needed to reckon my odds. Having initially been sobered with a five percent chance of survival over three years, factoring in my new variables I was now flitting about in the fifty to seventy-five percent range. But then I began weighing the odds that I should be alive to contract cancer in the first place. They made my original five percent prognosis appear lavish in comparison. For a time, it was all I could think about. So I did what ministers do when they can't get something out of their heads. I wrote a sermon about it.

ᏨᎧ

I am not, nor have I ever been, a betting man. Gambling claims no purchase on my soul. I say this not to boast. There is no virtue in abstaining from something that holds no fascination for you. Teetotalers who hate the taste of alcohol, nonsmokers who are allergic to smoke, and nonbettors who get no rush from games of chance do nothing to establish their virtue by not drinking, smoking, or gambling.

I demonstrated my lack of appetite for high-stakes gambling early. I was nine years old when I went with my parents to my one and only horse race—the Kentucky Derby. My father gave me ten dollars—a goodly sum back then—to bet until I lost it. At two dollars a race, I would be in the game for at least five of the nine races. He carefully pointed out to me that, unless I made some of it back—if I squandered, say, my stake on long shots that performed as expected—I would have nothing left in my pocket with which to place a bet on the Kentucky Derby itself, slated to take place near the end of the day's card.

I learned the lesson my father taught me a little too well perhaps. To limit my exposure, I would place a show bet on the horse that was favored to win. This far-from-daring strategy taught me one lesson that I have never forgotten. Even the most cautious gambler can lose. Some of the favorites staggered in out of the money, and even when they did perform as advertised each show bet on a low-odds winner earned me a slim dime or two on my two-dollar investment. No matter. By the time the Kentucky Derby rolled around, I still had five dollars in my pocket. Ready to do something daring, I put it all on Silky Sullivan.

Silky Sullivan was a western phenom. He stopped hearts in every race he entered by spotting his opponents a thirty-length lead. Halfway around the track, with the bunched contenders throwing up a great cloud of dust two city blocks ahead of him, Silky Sullivan loped along in solitary splendor, quixotic, romantic, and by every dint of racing logic, doomed. Then, to the amazement of all and delight of anyone who dared to dream, with a burst of awe-inspiring speed he would close in on the pack, catch it at the final turn, blow past one flagging pretender after another, pull up beside the leader, and win by a nose.

This was on western tracks, of course, not in the East. Silky would now be running against the best thoroughbreds in the land, not a bunch of pretty Californians. Even so, my young heart told me, win or lose, this was a horse worth every cent of my precious grubstake. So I placed five dollars on the long shot Silky Sullivan, not to win, of course—I wasn't that daring—but to show.

True to form, Silky ambled out of the gate and spotted a quarter furlong to the competition, prancing along nonchalantly until, like magic and flying like the wind, he closed the gap, dancing through the pack toward the flag. He's going to win, I screamed. This prophecy proved premature. Three horses crossed the finish line together. Valiant Silky, as I recall, closed in on the leaders, but just enough to eat their dust.

Silky Sullivan didn't break my heart that day. He made it beat faster. I'll never forget that cocky little horse. I can't tell you who won the 1958 Kentucky Derby. [I looked it up. It was Tim Tam.] But Silky Sullivan won a home in my personal Hall of Fame.

Lately I've been thinking quite a bit about life's odds. Four months ago I was diagnosed with what turned out to be a particularly savage form of esophageal cancer. Odds were, my doctor told me, that I had only months to live. Going onto the Internet—this does nothing, I might caution you, to boost the spirits of positive thinkers—confirmed this diagnosis in mind-numbing detail. Entering all my variables, as we knew them then, into the relevant actuarial tables, the odds were twenty to one against me.

My father died of cancer at fifty-nine. His father died at fifty-nine as well, of a heart attack. I am fifty-eight. The chapter I found myself opening offered compelling reason to believe it would likely be the last one in my book. And then I started beating the odds. Against all expectations, the cancer—though the tumor was large—had apparently not metastasized. Overnight, my odds leapt from twenty to one to fifty-fifty. A talented surgeon, Dr. Robert Korst, removed my esophagus, replacing it, conveniently, with my stomach. I now have what I call an estomagus. The post-op pathology brought us more good news. The margins were clear, the lymph nodes negative, and the tumor—right on the cusp between stage one and stage two—had barely penetrated the esophageal wall. New odds now: three to one that I am cured.

If there's a moral to this story—beyond the obvious one that I might usefully have quit drinking and smoking decades before I did, some seven years ago—it doesn't lie on the surface of these shifting odds. They are mere accidents, happy ones, it seems in my case, but accidents nonetheless. If my cancer returns to kill me, it won't be unfair, only unlucky, in the same sense that I was lucky to beat the odds that seemed at first to make survival a chancy bet. Beating the odds, I slowly began to realize, had nothing to do with the stakes of the mortality table. The truth of the matter struck me with tremendous force. I'd beaten the odds already, won the house on a zillions-to-one wager fifty-eight years before, the moment I was born. Think about it, and then translate this unaccountable triumph to your own precious life. Whether the odds that I will die at fifty-nine stand at twenty to one, fifty-fifty, or one to three is incidental, given how astronomically long the odds were against my being alive in the first place to reckon them.

There's a theological point here, one that gets lost in the haze of most salvation history. "What did I do to deserve this?" we ask when things turn against us, forgetting that we did nothing to deserve being placed in the way of trouble and joy in the first place. The odds against each one of us being here this morning are so

mind-staggering that they cannot be computed. Had I been paying more reverent attention, even a five percent chance that I
might live, not to mention outlive my father and grandfather,
should have found me dancing on the ceiling.

We're talking miracles here. Not an unlikely miracle, like God
parting the Red Sea for Moses to escape the Egyptians or stopping the sun for Joshua to win a battle, but the miracle of water itself, in which living organisms can incubate, and just enough
warmth and light from the sun to establish ideal conditions for
life to be nurtured and develop here on earth.

Consider the odds more intimately. Your parents had to couple at precisely the right moment for the one possible sperm to fer-
tilize the one possible egg that would result in your conception.
Right then, the odds were still a million to one against your being
the answer to the question your biological parents were con-
sciously or unconsciously posing. And that's just the beginning
of the miracle. The same unlikely happenstance must repeat itself
throughout the generations. Going back ten generations, this
miracle must repeat itself one thousand times—one and a quarter
million times going back only twenty generations. That's right.
From the turn of the twelfth century until today, we each have,
mathematically speaking, approximately two and a half million
direct ancestors. This remarkable pyramid turns in upon itself,
of course, with individual ancestors participating in multiple
lines of generation, until we trace ourselves back to when our ur-
ancestors, the founding couple, whom each one of us carries in
our bones, began the inexorable process that finally gave birth to
us all, kith and kin, blood brothers and sisters of the same mighty
mystery.

And that's only the egg and sperm part of the miracle. Remember, each of these ancestors had to live to puberty. For those
whose bloodline twines through Europe—and there were like
tragedies around the globe—not one of your millions of direct

forebears died as children during the great plague, for instance, which mowed down half of Europe with its mighty scythe.

There's a new book out on the *Mayflower*. It's a good book, telling a lively, unlikely tale. Five of my direct ancestors happened to be on that tiny boat, which brought the first band of doughty Pilgrims to our shores in 1620. Early in the book, I was brought up short when one of the five—remember, I wouldn't be here this morning without the unwitting assistance of all of them—twenty-four-year-old John Howland, an unmarried servant, fell off the *Mayflower* into the ocean halfway across the Atlantic. Miraculously he caught the rope his fellow Pilgrims threw overboard in their attempt to save him, and he lived. Had John Howland drowned, you might be hearing a better sermon this morning, but I, assuredly, would not be preaching it.

During their first winter in America, some fifty of the one hundred two original Pilgrims died. Among those who succumbed were my ancestors John and Elizabeth Tilley, but not their thirteen-year-old daughter, also named Elizabeth, or her ten-year-old friend Elizabeth Warren. Elizabeth Tilley went on to marry John Howland, establishing my mother's American line; Elizabeth Warren married Richard Church, establishing my father's. These accidents of survival, if nothing compared to the almost infinite odds against our winning billions of crapshoots in the sperm-and-egg stakes, are at least somewhat easier to grasp and existentially more meaningful to ponder.

By the way—and this is truly awesome, so awesome that it makes every salvation story in the world's great scriptures seem trivial in comparison—not only did all our human ancestors survive puberty to mate at the one and only instant that the requisite egg and sperm might connect to keep our tiny odds for arrival alive, but their prehuman ancestors did the same. Then we have to go back further to our premammalian ancestors; and back from there all the way to the ur-paramecium; and then, beyond that, to the pinball of planets and stars, playing out their agon into diurnal courses, spinning back through time to the big bang itself. Mathematically, our death is a simple inevitability, whereas our life hinges on an almost infinite sequence of perfect accidents. First a visible and then an invisible thread connects every one of us in an unbroken line genetically and kinetically to the instant of creation. Think about it. The universe was pregnant with us when it was born.

So what did we do to deserve this, whatever this might happen to be at any given moment in our life's unfolding saga? Please! The odds against our being here to ask that impertinent question beggar reckoning. Which is where the second element, accompanying awe in the fundamental religious equation, kicks into play: humility. Here is my favorite etymology: *human, humane, humanitarian, humility, humble, humus.* Dust to dust. And in between, erupting into consciousness—into pain and hope and trust and fear and grief and love—the miracle of life.

If you find yourself this morning out of the race, so far behind the pack that you can hardly see its dust—if the odds weigh against you, the odds against happiness returning to fill your days with joy, the seemingly overwhelming odds that you will never recover from whatever is bearing or beating you down—take a moment to ponder life's cosmic odds and how you've already beaten them. You, I, each one of us here this morning (or here anywhere this morning) have miraculously run our courses from the instant of creation to the advent of life on earth and on through billions of generations to reckon the privilege of looking out upon this magnificent morn.

And then, while you're blinking in the sun, pause one moment further and remember Silky Sullivan. A valiant stretch run may not make you a winner, but I can promise you this. It will make your heart and the hearts of those who love you beat faster. Believe me, there's nothing like a kick toward the flag to get the old blood pumping and the crowd off their bums cheering. Besides, without even trying, you've already won the only race that really matters. Unconsciously, yet omnipresent, you ran the gauntlet of stars and genomes to assume your full, nothing less than miraculous, place in the creation. Being alive to love and hurt, to fail and recover, to prove your grit and show compassion, that is life's true secret. Life's abiding opportunity, bequeathed against all odds to each and every one of us, is much the same: it is to live, and also to die, for the multitude of brothers and sisters who beat the odds with us, who labored with our ancestors' hands and wept tears (of grief and joy) from our ancestors' eyes, connecting us as kin to God and each other, blessed together, always together, with the privilege of running from gate to flag in life's glorious race.

❧

⌘ 15

Words to Live By

Between February 2007 and February 2008 I enjoyed one of the happiest and most productive years of my life. I finished a big, sweeping history of America's first culture war, *So Help Me God: The Founding Fathers and the First Great Battle over Church and State.* Harcourt brought it out in September to splendid reviews and I went out on the road, speaking in some twenty cities and lapping up all the free media I could secure. I'd long since accepted that I would likely never commit a best seller and *So Help Me God* didn't upset my expectations in that regard, but it was clearly one of my best books and I had great fun traveling about hawking it.

More importantly, my brush with death had brought our family closer together. We've always been a tightly knit group. In 1992 Carolyn and I brought four young children into our marriage and they melded remarkably into a close nuclear family. But my sickness was a catalyst for each of them, spurring them on to new endeavors with a greater sense of purpose, stretching their heartstrings, and leading us to a celebration of life and family that just didn't quit.

My renewed sense of well-being reminded me again of how much I had to give thanks for. Begin here. If you are healthy, give thanks for your heath. Anyone who is ailing will remind us what a blessing health is and how rarely we appreciate it while we are fortunate enough to possess it. There are millions of couples who can't conceive children, so we should always give thanks for our children if we have them, no matter how much trouble they may cause. And for parents. Parents, too, cause trouble, but without the miracle of having them, we wouldn't be around to complain. We might also give thanks for being able to walk, or the gifts of sight or hearing, if we are blessed with them; millions of people aren't, you know. As for our problems, why not be thankful for the sympathy of those who are concerned about our plight, whatever it may be. What could be finer or more welcome than to receive the love of everyone who loves us? Pray for the right things, often things you already have but tend to take for granted, and your prayers will come true.

"There is nothing that God hath established in a constant course of nature," writes John Donne, ". . . but would seem a Miracle, and exercise our admiration, if it were done but once." As I welcomed it now with new appreciation, take something as unexceptional as summer, a miracle parceled out to us only a limited number of times during our brief lifetime. If we were to taste but once of summer, of sultry days and verdant trees, of ice-cream trucks and frilly frocks, would we not be amazed by how miraculous summer is? Would we not embrace both June and one another, saying, "Look! Summer! Can you believe it? It's a miracle."

This insight lies at the heart of my mantra: want what you have; do what you can; be who you are. I circled back to it in a sermon I delivered right after brushfires ravaged Southern California in October 2007. My book tour had led me through Los Angeles and San Diego but a few days before tragedy struck.

⁊

I was in San Diego two weeks ago. It was a beautiful day, warm, not hot, the sky robin's egg blue. I had gone to Southern California, my new book in hand, sharing its message at churches and on talk shows. I remember how beautiful that day in San Diego was, because the top of the news, elbowing every other story to the periphery of people's consciousness, belied it. Out of the blue had come a terrible mudslide, destroying six houses in the San Diego foothills.

When I'm on the road, I watch more television than I do at home. I've discovered that it's possible to watch the very same news report over and over again, waiting for a tiny bit of new information, as if anything important were actually going to change. The night I arrived in San Diego, flipping through the news channels, it was "all mudslide all the time." I became quite familiar with the head of the geology department at San Diego State University, a dapper, articulate fellow with a handlebar mustache who knows the natural history of the entire San Diego Basin by heart.

The next morning, as I arrived at a local TV station to do my four-minute cameo, right there in the green room was San Diego's man of the hour. Since I was well versed in mudslides by this point, while we waited to be called into the studio I engaged him on the subject of natural catastrophes. "Here in Southern California," he said, "we pay for paradise by teetering precariously on the fault line for every natural disaster known to man. Earthquakes, mudslides, drought, wildfires. Even a volcano is waiting to blow. It keeps you humble," he said. "At least it should." As the ash came raining down over Southern California these past dramatic days, leaving its patina on more than a million disrupted lives, two thousand homes incinerated by indiscriminate flames, I thought back on my encounter with the wise old geologist.

One year ago this month, hit with a diagnosis of esophageal cancer, I was told I had but months to live. I stood, as it were, directly in the fire's path. Now, a year later, from my perch in the grandstand witnessing other people's tragedies as a concerned yet less implicated spectator, I had to pinch myself. "It keeps you humble. At least it should." When the roof caves in or a trapdoor swings, people who are allergic to all-purpose bromides, especially theological ones—"It was God's will, a part of God's plan,

and everything turns out for the best"—operate at something of
a disadvantage. As one who does not believe that God gave me
cancer before shifting his attention to Southern California where
he exercised his omnipotence by torching thousands of family
homes, I receive little comfort from the assurance that God
knows what he's doing when he plays with matches.

This week, I carried my message to Dallas and St. Paul.
Watching the fires rage with infernal beauty across my hotel TV
screen, I found myself reckoning the calculus of natural disaster.
In Minneapolis they are still talking about the terrible bridge col-
lapse that took dozens of lives last summer. But all eyes were now
on California. In Los Angeles and San Diego, this week's wildfires
were hundreds of times as devastating as the mudslides in San
Diego that had ruled the airwaves just two weeks before. For
another exponential contrast, scroll back to Katrina, which destroyed one hundred times again as many homes. Even my air-
plane book gave me no respite. Between Minneapolis and New
York, half of its protagonists died of the Black Plague.

So where is God in all of this? Commingled, I believe, with
the victims' tears. God doesn't torch houses, will entire cities to
disappear under the floodwaters, or sentence toddlers to drown
who wander too close to the family pool. I could not worship such
a God, even if I believed in him. But I don't believe in him. My
God is not a puppet master pulling every string above this tiny
globe as if the universe turned on how we behave here. Greater
than all and yet present in each, no less mysterious than the creation itself, God is not the cause of our undoing but the cosmic
ground of our being. I've never needed biblical miracles to con-
firm my faith. It's not the supernatural, but the super in the natural, that I celebrate. I draw strength and insight from the Bible
and embrace Jesus's two great commandments (love to God and
love to neighbor) as my own, but following the spirit, not the
letter, of the Scriptures, my abiding touchstones are awe and hu-

mility. Death, I have said time and again from this pulpit, is not life's enemy. With birth, it is the hinge on which life as we know it—each individual unique, ephemeral, and therefore precious—turns.

Every minister who's paying the slightest bit of attention spends a lifetime preparing for death's exam. A year ago this month, just how strong the theological foundation I had built for myself met the test. With compelling reason to believe that my number had been called, I finally had a chance to see if the balm I had brought over the years to the bedsides of your loved ones would salve my own fresh wound.

During the days after my diagnosis, through my brain, as if on a Möbius loop, cycled my theological mantras.

> Religion is our human response to the dual reality of being alive and having to die.
>
> We are the religious animal; knowing that we must die, we cannot help but question what life means.
>
> We are more alike in our ignorance than we differ in our knowledge.
>
> *God* is not God's name. *God* is our name for that which is greater than all and yet present in each.
>
> Whether or not there is life after death, surely there is love after death.
>
> The one thing that can never be taken from us, even by death, is the love we give away before we die.
>
> The purpose of life is to live in such a way that our lives will prove worth dying for.

One year later, each of these propositions stands unchallenged at the heart of my faith. Yet they are not what got me through my time of trial. The consolation they offered was intellectual, not emotional. My soul needed something more bracing than my own soaring rhetoric. So I returned to the mantra by which I have attempted to guide my life since shortly after 9/11: want what you have; do what you can; be who you are.

Let me unpack these words to live by in reverse order. First, be who you are. Easier said than done, I admit, but essential to peace of mind and true success in life.

Being who we are means embracing our God-given nature and talents. I, for instance, loved my father. I still love my father. I honor and admire him. Once, however, I wanted, more than anything, to borrow his ladder to the stars. I had more confidence in him than I did in myself. I wanted to be like him, not like me. Then the moment of reckoning arrived. Halfway through my doctoral work, I was handed a political career on a platter. In 1976, at the age of twenty-seven, I had run my father's presidential campaign in Nebraska, a primary he won against Jimmy Carter. After the primary season ended, the Carter people invited me to head up their Nebraska effort that fall, sweetened by an offer from Nebraska's lieutenant governor to remain in the state as vice-chair of the Democratic Party, with the promise of standing for Congress two years later if everything worked out. I might very well have done this, but my father interceded. He called me a quitter. Finish your doctorate, he said. Then go ahead and do whatever you wish with your life. So I persevered. And, in persevering, I found my calling. Two years later, I was installed as the ninth minister of All Souls. For almost thirty years I have been privileged to serve this congregation, fulfilling not my destiny— I don't believe in destinies—but answering a call that was mine, not someone else's. To envy another's skills, looks, or gifts rather than embracing your own nature and call is to fail in two respects. In trying unsuccessfully to be who we aren't, we fail to become who we are.

No less important than being who you are is doing what you can. This, too, is more difficult than it sounds. How much wasted energy we spend trying to do what we can't. And how often we fail to optimize our efforts and thereby achieve the significant goals that do lie within our power. When we quit trying because we fail to achieve our pipe dreams, we overlook all we actually could accomplish by putting our shoulder squarely to the right wheel. To do what you can is to do all you can, not less, not more.

Finally, and most pointedly for me last year when I was diagnosed with cancer, want what you have. Did I want cancer? Of course not, but to obsess on the bad things that befall us squeezes out a just appreciation for the good. The time we waste on wishful thinking or regret detracts from the time we might devote to being grateful for all that is ours, here and now, to savor and embrace. When I was sick I remembered to want nothing more than the caring affection of those who loved me. Wanting what I had, my prayers were answered.

In each of our lives not only will some rain fall, but fires will burn, the ground will shake, and one day, life itself will be exacted in payment for the gift of life bestowed. By wanting what we have, doing what we can, and being who we are, our cup will forever be half full, not half empty. Do these same things with reverence, humbled by awe, and our cup runneth over.

The alternative, to long for what we lack—for things we have lost or shall likely never find—offers little save the sour pleasures of victimhood and regret. Fantasy is no better. Wishful thinking is both sloppy and sentimental. We should think to wish instead for things a little closer at hand.

> The courage to bear up under pain
> The grace to take our successes lightly
> The liberation that comes with forgiveness
> The energy to address tasks that await our doing
> The meaning to be found in giving ourselves to others
> The patience to surmount things that are dragging us down
> The joy to be gained in even the smallest endeavor

The wonder that lies between the sacred moments of our birth
and death

I call this thoughtful wishing—wishing for what is ours, here and
now, to have, do, and be.

❧

The Death Sentence

The sky is pale pure blue
through the gray bony branches
of the wintered tree
outside the arching church window
through which I stare
this Sunday
while the quiet
congregation listens
to our minister
telling us he won't
be here to see this tree,
or any tree,
next year.

How to hold this sorrow?
With smiles and tears
we stand and sing to honor his life's song.

—"A Minister Says Goodbye," Alice Kenner, February 3, 2008

On the first day of February, I discovered that my cancer had returned with a vengeance. The clock was now ticking more loudly and clearly than before. But we, as a family, having gone through all the preliminaries, were ready. In the meantime, my eldest son Frank and I had gotten a partial-season-ticket package to watch our beloved Mets. Nina had returned from England with her fiancé, Tom Adams, and launched into a wonderful career at American

Express. Carolyn's eldest son, Jacob, had joined Mayor Bloomberg's staff, with a fine, challenging portfolio. And Nathan had changed schools and career paths, demonstrating great seriousness and winning excellent grades at Colorado State University. Carolyn, too, was moving from strength to strength, both in her career and in her important advocacy work on behalf of women and minorities in business. Above all, as a family we had done some good, hard work together. Having circled the wagons once, we knew what we were doing this time when forced to circle them again. So we hunkered down to confront the task at hand.

All that remained was to tell my congregation. Knowing full well how much spiritual energy my parishioners had staked on my return to health, this task proved harder than I could have imagined. Two days later, I stood before my congregation, told them of my cancer's return, and then—casting my eye forward—preached another version of my now well-practiced sermon, "Love and Death."

℘

One of our longtime members, Damon Brant, has compiled a stunning book of photographs, a series of candid portraits that he took of his father in his deathbed, with nurses and family at the bedside or waiting in the wings. Called simply, "Hospice," and free of textual adornment, Damon's unsentimental yet deeply moving record touches the heart. Why does it move those who never knew Damon's father? Because his death is our death too. We are never closer than when we ponder the great mystery that beats at the heart of our shared being.

At every deathbed, the light that shines is framed by darkness. When those we love die, a part of us dies with them. When those we love are sick, we too feel the pain. Yet all of this is worth it. Especially the pain. Grief and death are sacraments, or can be. A sacrament symbolizes communion, the act of bringing us together. To comfort another is to bring her our strength. To console is to be with him in his aloneness. To commiserate is to share her pain.

The act of releasing a loved one from all further obligations as he lies dying—to tell him it's all right, that he is safe, that we love him and he can go now—is life's most perfect gift, the final expression of unconditional love.

Unless we armor our hearts, we cannot protect ourselves from loss. We can only protect ourselves from the death of love. Yet without love, nothing matters. Break your life into a million pieces and ask yourself what of any real value might endure after you are gone. The pieces that remain will each carry love's signature. Without love, we are left only with the aching hollow of regret, that haunting emptiness where love might have been.

Such is the story that unfolds frame by frame in Damon's book. A man is dying. He has been given but a few sweet days to live. His wife and children gather at his bedside. They reminisce. They hold hands. They laugh. They cry. They wait. Their hearts tremble with love.

Damon's pictures tell life's deepest story. They invite us to enter the sacred realm of the heart.

The realm of the heart is not only where we touch each other most sacredly; it is also the place where we encounter the cosmic source for our sense of awe. What a luxury we enjoy, wondering what will happen after we die. Having spent billions of years in gestation, present in all that preceded us—fully admitting the pain and difficulty involved in actually being alive, able to feel and suffer, grieve and die—we can only respond in one way: with gratitude. And how does this affect the way we treat others? I hope it means we will treat others as being as unpredictable, unexpectable, and amazing as we are. In the womb of the universe when God first gave birth, they, too, have run a billion billion gauntlets, emerging against almost impossible odds to walk here beside us on this planet. They are more than neighbors. They are kin, honest to God and hope to die kin.

Religion does its best (and worst) work here. Not in the creation chapter or the Armageddon chapter, but in the middle of the story, when all the actors are thrown together, struggling for meaning, none knowing as much as we pretend, think, or wish we knew. The wisest of all teachers tells us, "Love God. Love your neighbor as yourself." Even, "Love your enemy." He instructs us to love our brother, even if he doesn't know that he is our brother. Love our sister, even if she doesn't know that she is our sister. Exchange pride for humility. Forgive without ceasing. And judge actions but not people, remembering—I would add—that somewhere they and we share at least one common ancestor who, with twenty-twenty foresight, would do the same for us if she were here.

In fact, she is here. Those who have come before us must now use our hands to touch, our eyes to see. We carry them in our hearts and bones, we and our blood brothers and sisters, survivors of the ongoing miracle, never ceasing to amaze, pouring itself into new vessels, re-creating itself, over and over again.

We see little of the road ahead or the sky above. And the dust we raise clouds our eyes, leaving only brief interludes to contemplate the stars. All we can do, every now and again, is to stop for a moment and look.

Look. Morning has broken and we are here, you and I, breathing the air, admiring the slant sun as it refracts through these magnificent, pellucid windows and dances in motes of dust above the pews, calling us to attention, calling us homeward.

Dust to dust.

Heart to heart.

❧

Where Is God?

From the moment I first got sick, well-meaning people have been peppering me with cure-alls. I should go to Basel or Stockholm or Mexico City to avail myself of some brilliant doctor's cure. I should try this herb or that diet. Well-meaning individuals send me doubtless very fine books with titles like *Remarkable Recovery* and *How to Fight Cancer and Win.* Or they tell me what page to crack my Bible open to. Psalm 103 promises that God "heals all diseases." And the New Testament assures us that "with God nothing shall be impossible."

In short, if I die, I fail. That's the bottom line for all such thinking. If I die, I didn't fight smart enough. I didn't expect a miracle.

It is human nature to pray for miracles, so much so that some of us think to pray only when nothing short of a miracle can save us, a net to break our fall or an angel to sweep down and catch us in her arms. The Russian novelist Ivan Turgenev went so far as to claim that every time we pray, we pray for a miracle. "Every prayer reduces itself to this," he said: "'Great God, grant that twice two be not four.'"

Sometimes twice two is not four. We have all known such apparent miracles in our lives. A loved one awakens from a yearlong coma. The cancer riddling a friend's body goes into sudden, complete remission. Such things happen just often enough that it might seem foolish not to throw a Hail Mary pass with two seconds left and one's life on the line. There is no shame in this.

When the bombs come hailing down, an atheist has the right to blurt out, "God save me," from his foxhole. Whether or not God takes a hand in arranging the shrapnel, the atheist may miraculously emerge unscathed, which is certainly worth the intellectual compromise of a final desperate prayer.

But to pray for God to heal what all my doctors now assure me is indeed terminal cancer is a different matter entirely. Such prayers may be answered, but likely the answer won't be yes. It will be "Get real."

The question remains, if I did pray to God to cure my cancer, why shouldn't God answer my prayer? I could issue a formal complaint that should carry at least a little weight in a divine court of law. Why fate me, a relatively young man, never to meet my grandchildren and not to grow old beside my darling wife?

Once we begin asking such questions, they do not stop. Why did five children in Queens perish in a recent fire? Why did a tornado pick worship hour on Sunday morning to hit a church in South Carolina, killing the minister's four-year-old daughter? What had he done to anger God? Don't you think he asked himself that question? Better to have asked what had she done—she and her thousands of brothers and sisters who died in the recent tsunami in Asia—to deserve so untimely and brutal a sentence of death.

When the bottom falls out of the world, when a mighty wave slaps the life out of everyone they love, leaving them bereft and alone amid the ruins, some believers challenge the nature of reality with the reality of their own experience and lose their faith. After the 2004 tsunami, "This disaster has shaken my faith," one bishop dared to confess. Of course it had. Look for a loving God in the eye of a hurricane or riding the crest of a tsunami and, barring the most inhumane twists of logic imaginable, you will look in vain.

In fact, if such a God exists, then God is a bastard. The traditional Western God—the Lord of heaven and earth, all-knowing and all-powerful, the deus ex machina driving human history, treating men and women as wanton boys treat flies—is either a bastard or a sturdy figment of our theological imaginations.

I simply can't believe in any God who, on the day after Christmas, would choose to rip the earth asunder, welling the tide to life-crushing heights, and then, with his all-seeing eye, watch it crash down on more than a thousand beaches to claim more than one hundred times that many souls. Tens of thousands of orphans. As many heart-shattered widows, widowers, and parents combing snapshots of mangled bodies for a last look at their loved ones. Most of them poor to begin with, now impoverished beyond all measure. However insurance companies may choose to define them, whatever *acts of God* may be for actuarial purposes, the one thing acts of God surely are not is acts of God.

The logic of those who view God as the world's puppet master is simple, if brutal. Whether in regard to natural or personal disasters (from tsunamis to terminal cancer), if God is pulling all the strings that entangle us, then God must be furious with us. If death seizes our loved ones from us, then we must have done something wrong or they must have done something wrong for God to punish us all so severely.

We follow this logic almost instinctively when something terrible happens to us. To find higher meaning in that which has destroyed all the meaning we have come to know and trust, we ask the unanswerable question, "Why?" Why this, why me, why now? We struggle to make sense of God's will. We attempt to comfort one another by drowning our ignorance in God's knowledge: "God knows best," we parrot to one another. Or, "God has his reasons." Or, "It is all part of God's divine plan."

So understood, God's will is a frightening and demeaning concept. Acts of God become themselves ungodly acts. We surrender our will at the altar of an arbitrary, all-mighty, and merciless magistrate. We place our trust in the hands of one who has destroyed our trust. We submit our hearts to one who has torn our hearts to pieces. When our experience of reality renders traditional conceptions of God to be blasphemous—all-knowing, all-mighty, and therefore, at times, all-cruel—we have two choices. Either we conclude that there is no God, or we reimagine the divine to reencompass our experience of what we believe to be truly holy.

Over the years, I have traveled the long road from religious skepticism to an abiding faith. Back in the 1970s, even once I began preaching, I avoided invoking God almost entirely. It embarrassed me. Above all, I didn't want anyone to mistake what I might mean by *God* for the tiny, judgmental, anthropomorphic God of so many true believers. I believed only in things I could parse and thereby comprehend. I approached the creation as a taxidermist, not a worshipper. Even the most fragile and beautiful manifestations of the creation, I examined as a blindered lepidopterist might a butterfly. I netted, chloroformed, and mounted them for observation. After long study of my favorite specimens, I could only conclude that butterflies can't fly.

Challenged by the demands of love and death, I had to make room in my theology for a more capacious, if unfathomable, power. I had to clear a place for mystery on the altar of my hearth, which before I had crowded with icons to knowledge. The eighteenth-century classical lithographs of architectural drawings that I favored while at divinity school could no longer divert my awareness from the cracking plaster behind them and between. I needed something far more arresting and humbling, something more like Vincent Van Gogh's *Starry Night*.

I soon discovered, whenever I wished to soar a little higher into the mystery of the heavens or dive a little deeper into the unfathomable sea of being, I lacked the vocabulary necessary to describe such a journey. Stripped of religious symbol, my attempts at poetry were at best prosaic. Of greater concern, without transcendental symbols to relate the sublime to the ordinary, my spiritual life was parched, my well of inspiration dry. Only by sacrificing a bit of pride, and petty pride at that, could I even begin to commune with the muses or touch an angel's wing.

So it was, haltingly at first and then with slowly gathering confidence, I began to employ God-talk. I also returned to the Scriptures, listening with my Hebrew forebears for the still, small voice, and heeding Jesus's teaching that the realm of God is here, right now, within us, in our very midst. Through parable and paradox, seeking evidence of the divine in the ordinary, I began to uncover little hints of eternity in time.

Albert Schweitzer spoke of this principle as reverence for life. We are a part of, not apart from, a vast and mysterious living system. Mystics of every faith proclaim this sense of oneness. Thus the Brahman-Atman relationship of Hinduism, the sense of nirvana of the Buddhists, and the concept of Jesus that "I and the Father are One." All of these are examples of mystical oneness. The great religious seers have all recognized that beyond the intellectual realm lies a numinous oneness that transcends all differences, call it the Holy, the divine Spirit, God—it doesn't matter. The mystic oneness of person to person, of mother to child and then brother to sister, is but a simple expression of the greater mystical oneness of all existence in the great chain of being. Such religion exalts self and other alike by placing us together in divine kinship as children of one great mystery, children of God the mother, creator, consoler, and comforter.

There is nothing novel, and certainly nothing blasphemous, about reimagining God. Responding to life-and-death questions, we have reinvented and thereby rediscovered the Holy throughout the centuries. Consider our ancestors, the searchers who came before us. Begin with cave dwellers—hunters and gatherers—for whom the greatest imaginable powers were forces of nature. "God" was manifest to them in lightning and in thunder, perhaps even in the game they hunted for sustenance. When agriculture replaced hunting and gathering, these deities became female. Power now lay in reaping and sowing, in the turning of the seasons.

Fecundity determined survival, "God" became "Goddess"; pro-creation, creation; birth, life.

Later, with the city-state, power came wrapped in the robes of authority. "God" was now Lord or King, protector, enforcer, and judge. A breakthrough in this view of the divine nature arrived with the Hebrews, who believed that their God and King was the only God and King. Less an imperialistic than an ethical development, this led them to attribute their failures not to another stronger God, but to their own shortcomings. With Jesus, God became Father (in fact, Daddy, or "Abba"), a far more intimate authority figure.

In Western society, the God most unbelievers reject is the traditional Judeo-Christian God: ostensibly merciful and just, yet also demanding, capricious on occasion, and sometimes cruel. Aided by the Copernican revolution, for many thoughtful people this God was overthrown centuries ago. As has happened many times before, God was not therefore dead; "God" was reimagined. When Copernicus displaced us from the center of the universe, in reimagining God one group of scientists and theologians seized upon a metaphor better suited to their new worldview. Enter God the Watchmaker, who created the world, set it ticking, and then withdrew to another corner of the cosmos. This is the God of the deists, a God icy and remote, still transcendent but no longer personal.

Today, we witness a further revolution, one as profound as that initiated by Copernicus and Galileo half a millennium ago. From quantum physics to cosmology, scientific students of the creation have become masters of paradox. Postmodern philosophers contemplate the dynamic relationship between how we say something and what we mean. Political theorists speak of a global empire whose emperor, though virtual, not factual, is no less powerful and real. And theologians entertain notions of divinity no longer encumbered by static concepts such as omniscience and omnipotence. Having moved from one transcendent God to another (first Lord and Judge, then absentee landlord), we are beginning to encounter what might best be called a reflexive God, cocreator with us in an unfolding, intricate drama of hitherto unimaginable complexity. This God is not immutable, but ever changing, reaching, and growing, even as we change, reach, and grow. Such a God may even grieve when we grieve. As we expand the compass of our empathy, God ennobles our suffering into a sacrament. No longer merely actors on God's stage, by this reading of creation history, we are participants in the scripting of God's drama.

The surest path to God (the Sacred or the Holy) is to follow not the logic of our minds but the logic of our hearts. All of us suffer. We are broken and in need of healing. We struggle to accept ourselves and forgive others. Aware of our imperfections, we seek more perfect faith, hope, and justice. At our best, we feel our love in others' hearts and rise together in answer to the urgings of conscience. We discover the Holy—its healing and saving power—by acting in harmony. Remember, *God* is simply our name for the highest power we know. If we define God as love—as good a definition as any—we discover God's nature in our personal experience of love. This may not mean God is actually love, but it certainly suggests that love is divine.

We are born into a great mystery. We die into a great mystery. In between—in that little dash between the dates on our tombstone—what we know of God we learn from love's lessons. Love teaches us the difference between what is holy and what is diabolical. When we act in concert with our higher selves and embrace our neighbors, we act in the presence of all that is divine. Conversely, the demonic divides us against our higher selves and from our neighbor. Whatever is born of hatred and division is not of God, but only that which truly saves, that which is born of love and compassion. So understood, God is not all-knowing or all-powerful, but all-loving and all-merciful. When love dwells in our hearts, we dwell in God's presence.

Does this answer the question "Why?" No, it doesn't. Final answers to ultimate questions lie far beyond the ken of human understanding. We keep asking, of course. It's the nature of our being, the nature of our quest. We keep climbing up to reach the stars even as God comes down to share our tears, each to the other like a vanishing pot of gold at two ends of a rainbow. The mystery is, by reaching for God—for a divine hand that may turn out not to be there—we can in fact be changed, even saved. And in seeking us out, who knows? Perhaps God, too, is changed. Humbled. Spun into webs of passion and stung with pain. Brought to life.

Life after Death

In 1998 my family and I went on a ten-day adventure to Egypt, one of the cradles of civilization. The earliest tomb we visited was near the ancient city of Memphis. More than forty-five hundred years old and belonging to an important nobleman, its walls were covered with depictions of domestic life, of dancing and dining. One wall showed jugglers and acrobats; another, children at play. Inside was a map of the tomb, giving instructions to the gods on where to find the crypt containing its occupant's mummified remains. Sufficient food was stored to provide sustenance for a long journey, and all his treasures filled the chambers as in later tombs. But the distinguishing features here, the winning touches, were joyous representations of life on earth, children playing, mother and infant, lavish feasts, and but a very few gods.

However careful his plans—and they were manifestly elaborate—I wonder whether this nobleman was ready for death when the hour came. His preparations were meticulous—the heavenly traffic signs and assembled stores—but was he ready to journey across the sacred waters? Was he better prepared than the slaves who built his tomb, who cut the stones, affixing them so closely that the elements could not invade his sacred sanctuary to disturb his progress or his peace? Was he better prepared than the artisans who carved dancing children, acrobats, jugglers, venison, and amphorae filled with flowing wine on the walls of his sepulcher? For all his power and riches, was this nobleman ready to entrust his heart to the embalmer? More ready than you or I?

All I know is this. Religion starts here. It starts at the entrance to the tomb.

No one knows whether heaven actually exists. All we can say with any confidence about the afterlife is that it cannot be any stranger or more unexpected than life before death. The least prepared pilgrim could not be more startled by heaven the moment following death than a preternaturally prescient embryo would be astounded by life on earth the moment following birth. Nonetheless, we can learn something about the appropriateness of our earthly desires from the images we create of heaven. Many of them really are quite silly, an eternity of harps, halos, and hymnals, the heavenly hosts fluffed up on clouds singing hosannas forever. Whatever happens after we die, I hope it isn't this. So defined, heaven might best be described as punishment for good behavior.

Religious literature is rich with less descriptive yet more evocative views of heaven. Plato speaks of "jewels of the soul" that we perceive "through a glass dimly" as the most valuable prizes on our human treasure hunt. Saint Paul may have had this passage in mind when he wrote, "Now we see through a glass darkly, then face to face." "Surely unto God all things come home," affirms the Koran. "Our rendezvous is fitly appointed," Walt Whitman writes. "God will be there and wait till we come." Or, as that fine old spiritual beckons, sounding from the fields of oppression, facing death we sing the song of liberation: "Swing low, sweet chariot, coming for to carry me home."

Heaven or no, the great teachers of religion and philosophy tend to take their own advice and therefore die quite well. Untroubled on the eve of his death, the Buddha comforted his disciples by reminding them that they didn't need him in order to find peace. "Be ye lamps unto yourselves," he preached in his farewell sermon. "Hold to the truth within yourselves as the only lamp." Socrates accepted his own death sentence with equal equanimity. "The difficulty, my friends, is not to avoid death, but to avoid evil; for it runs faster than death ... Those who believe death to be a calamity are in error." And (following the example of Jesus) Sir Thomas More forgivingly assured his tearful executioner while mounting the scaffold, "Quiet yourself, good Master Pope, and be not discomforted; for I trust that we shall, once in Heaven, see each other full merrily where we shall be sure to live and love together, in joyful bliss eternally." The Buddha, Socrates, and Sir Thomas More each held different views of the afterlife, but all were equally at peace with death.

For me, to be at home with God right here and now is—as they say—to die and go to heaven. It may be all of heaven we will ever know. I certainly don't believe in hell. I am a Universalist. However bad I may have been at times, the God I believe in is too good to sentence me (or any of God's creatures) to eternal damnation. I am confident that when we die, we will all experience peace.

This faith is buttressed by studies conducted of people who have been presumed dead and then, through extreme medical measures, brought back to life. Many experience a taste of the afterlife, hovering over their bodies, flowing into and through a great tunnel of light, met at its end by loved ones who have died before them. The patterns of these memories are remarkably similar. No one is eager to return to life. Their experience of the beyond is completely peaceful. They are enveloped in a divine embrace.

What is going on here? Perhaps the body conspires with us at our moments of greatest exigency, rushing endorphins into our bloodstream, giving us a natural, psychedelic high to go out on. That still doesn't explain hovering over our bodies, seeing doctors and nurses rush in and out of the operating room, dispassionately overhearing their frantic conversations, watching them try to save our lives.

What these experiences suggest to me is that the trauma of death may, in certain instances, release all our latent powers. I can only presume that we live trapped in our bodies, exercising only some tiny percent of our psychic potential. ESP experiences and moments of déjà vu suggest the same. Consciousness is more powerful an instrument than the wisest and most spiritually actualized among us begins to tap. The other possibility these stories suggest is really no less likely. There is a heaven. When we die, we shuck off our earthly coil, look back without nostalgia, and sail away to forever through a tunnel of light.

Whichever interpretation best fits your science, theology, or fancy, my two points of confidence regarding death remain. First, there is no hell. In none of the life-after-life experiences do people return with panicked tales of devils waving pitchforks at them. And, second, death is peaceful, so peaceful that those who wake up from it don't want to return to their bodies to fight another day.

The peace of extinction is different from the peace of fulfillment, of course. Yet, whether to fulfillment or extinction, when God carries us home it will be to a place of eternal rest. No promise is more comforting and none, for me, more certain. Put in theological terms, we come from God and return to God, even if only as a postanimate (as before we were a preanimate) part of the body of the creation. Having passed through the valley of the shadow of death, we will dwell in the house of the Lord forever.

Since theology is poetry, not science, let me cede the last word on this subject to a poet. One who sat at William Blake's bedside when Blake was dying reported that "just before he died, his countenance became fair, his eyes brightened, and he burst into singing of the things he saw in Heaven." Blake was a true visionary. He also saw the trees outside his window filled with angels when he was but a boy of seven.

Does that mean angels really exist? Who knows. It is impossible to prove the existence of angels without leaving their realm. Like God, angels are beyond proof. Once we start arguing about whether or not angels exist, we have already missed the point.

I will venture this, however. When angels dance on the head of a pin, they don't concern themselves with how many can fit, as if they were crowding into a phone booth. Their full attention is devoted to the joy of the dance.

ᘒ 19

Saying Goodbye

I'm not any better at saying goodbye than I am with sad movies. Born sunny-side up, I want all my endings to be happy ones. That may, in part, explain my lifelong attempt to reclaim death as the most natural thing imaginable, a well-planted period or, in some rare instants, an exclamation mark placed at the end of our life story.

My time of final farewells is still, prospectively, a few months off. I go back and forth from chemo to my writing, thankful for the steroids they give me to help me tolerate the poison they're pumping into my body. I wake up fresh as a daisy at two in the morning and rush to my writing couch to work on another chapter. (The writing couch is not a new innovation, by the way. The way I compensate for my natural indolence while working is to work lying down.)

One thing I do know is that we can't say goodbye to those we love either too early or too often. "I love you" should end every farewell, howsoever briefly we plan to be apart. Death can pounce in the middle of the night or interrupt the most uneventful day. When this happens, what a relief it is that the last message we imparted to our loved one was "I love you."

Actual goodbyes, when we know someone is dying, are different, of course. When my father-in-law, Earle Buck, was dying of pancreatic cancer (struck by the same disease that finally took my father's life), my mother-in-law asked me, "When should I say goodbye to Earle?" We knew he was ready to go, but we don't die on cue any more than our mothers were able to give birth on cue. Still, I said to Minna, "Say goodbye every time you leave him. Tell him if he goes before you return, that is fine. And, of course, tell him that you love him."

Strangely, perhaps, our loved ones need our permission to die in peace. Not only in medical circles is death considered a failure. A father, say, may feel that he is abandoning his wife and family, no longer taking care of them as he should. His death is an affront to his sense of duty. Every time his wife says, "What will we ever do without you?" meaning no doubt to let him know how much he's loved, he may hear something very different, like, "Please don't leave us holding the bag." So goodbyes are complicated. When the time comes near, we should never say, "Please don't go," but rather give our full permission, cheer them on, tell them it's almost over now, that they can make it, that we're rooting for them.

My wife, Carolyn, had the most astounding insight when her father was dying. "Giving death is a lot like giving birth," she said. "After hours of labor, we circled my dad's bedside saying one version or another of 'Push, push,' all the way through his death rattle. You're doing great, we told him. You're almost there. Just a little more work and you will reach the peace you've been dreaming of. We love you. We love you."

Just like giving birth: "Push, push." "You can do it." "One more time."

Because they gave him permission, my father-in-law knew that it was okay for him to go. He wouldn't be letting anyone down.

Earlier goodbyes, during the months one is dying, are in a way more complicated. Neither I nor my loved ones wish to bring a pall over our every conversation by speaking of my impending death. But they, I know, want the chance openly to express their feelings without disturbing mine. For me, the slightly perverse desire to conquer death can tempt me to approach it like a beautiful, snowy day in December, or a valedictory walk in Central Park. For the sake of everyone who loves you, I don't recommend this approach. I myself do my best to avoid practicing it. There is, however, a happy medium between avoidance and obsessing. Take those who love you, one at a time, and sit down and ask them how they're feeling about your death. Then shut your mouth and listen.

This is part of the unfinished business that my wife was talking about when I boasted of having finished mine. We may finally each die alone, but even to the extent that we are islands, which is very slight indeed, we are each part of an archipelago. So I sit down with my daughter and ask her how she's feeling about my death. She pours her heart out. It is breaking in two. She weeps through her words. I can't comfort her. I don't even try, because making her feel better about my death is, I know, only a way for me to make things better that can't be made better. Letting people grieve is simply another way to let them love you. It's not your fault that you are dying. Don't make it your fault that they are grieving. And don't make it their fault that they openly mourn that you will never hold their babies in your arms. Thank them for it. Bless their tears. Tell them they mean the world to you. And before you know it, you will be crying, too, for them, for you, for the whole aching world.

Being open to others' grief gives your loved ones the opportunity to tell you directly, not only after you are gone, how much they love and value you, how they see you, and how they see themselves keeping your memory alive. Such farewells, which happen well before we go, are as cathartic as funerals. If tears water the soul, they also buoy the heart. Crying is one of the most beautiful things two people can do together. And don't worry. It won't go on forever. We run out of tears, when we've spent the tears we must. Besides, as often as not in one of these "tell me how you're really feeling conversations," the tears of grief will soon, for some saving, silly reason, turn into tears of laughter. You will then feel better, but so will she. How much finer this joint catharsis is than its sad, familiar opposite: for your loved ones to cry in your absence and laugh in your presence, simply because they don't want to make you feel bad.

Some people, of course, can make it all the way through their lifetime without ever once showing their feelings. The advent of death will be unlikely to change that. Sometimes, to honor a dying loved one, the best we can do is cry by ourselves. But the hardest cases may crack with death's approach. Tolstoy's immortal story, the death of Ivan Illich, tells of one such man, who holds his feelings in tight to the very end. Only when he can no longer speak does his mind flood with everything he so longs to pour out of his heart, his love and gratitude, his need for forgiveness. In this short, poignant tale, Ivan's wife and daughter walk in and out of his room unaware of his final blessings. It is the purest of all tragedies.

As always, I am preaching to myself here. I express my love openly but not as intimately as I might wish, making me a tough customer for loved ones to say goodbye to. My love is strong and real, but I temper it by a concomitant need to ensure that everyone around me is happy. The plain truth is, death is not a happy occasion, certainly not for those who will be left behind. So I turn for my goodbye lessons to my wife and children. They are my teachers now. I do everything in my power to enter the circle of their pain.

I may even have won yet another reprieve. As these pages go to press, the chemo regimen I am under appears to be working. My first post-treatment CT scan showed major shrinkage in all the tumors. This particular form of cancer is not curable, but with successful therapy, as I seem to be receiving, its ravages can be postponed. I shall happily renew my lease on life with each new offering sheet.

When it does come time for me to die, I may still, in extremis, close down like my father did and hold everyone at bay. I hope not, but I may. However surrounded we may be by love, we each die alone. And who knows, part of the process of dying may encourage us to release ourselves from all our earthly bonds so that we may leave in greater peace.

This is one chapter I will have to leave unfinished. I won't know how it ends, until I say my final goodbyes.

Love after Death

After death our bodies may be resurrected. Our souls may transmigrate or become part of the heavenly pleroma. We may join our loved ones in heaven. Or we may return the constituent parts of our being to the earth from which it came and rest in eternal peace. About life after death, no one knows. But about this we surely know: there is love after death. Not only do our finest actions invest life with meaning and purpose, but they also live on after us. Two centuries from now, the last tracings of our being will yet express themselves in little works of love that follow bead by bead in a luminous catena extending from our dear ones out into their world and then on into the next, strung by our own loving hands.

Death is love's measure. Not only is our grief when someone dies testimony to our love, but when we ourselves die, the love we have given to others is the one thing death can't kill. Only our unspent love dies when we die, love unspent because of fear. It is fear that locks love in the prison of our hearts, there to be buried with us.

"Love is the reconciliation of man with God," the German theologian and martyr Dietrich Bonhoeffer once wrote. "The disunion of men with God, with other men, with the world and with themselves, is at an end. Man's origin is given back to him." Bonhoeffer spent the final years of his short life in prison, awaiting execution for having knowledge of the assassination plot against Adolf Hitler. Pondering there both the love of enemies and the pain of separation from his loved ones, by drawing on his faith Bonhoeffer did something really quite remarkable. He found room within his prison cell for his heart to flourish. Bonhoeffer's receptivity to grace finds eloquent expression in one of the last letters he wrote before he died. He sent it to his fiancée, Maria von Wedemeyer-Weller, just before Christmas in 1944.

These will be quiet days in our homes. But I have had the experience over and over again that the quieter it is around me, the clearer do I feel the connection to you. It is as though in solitude the soul develops senses that we hardly know in everyday life. Therefore I have not felt lonely or abandoned for one moment. You, the parents, all of you, the friends and students of mine at the front, all are constantly present to me. Your prayers and good thoughts, words from the Bible, discussion long past, pieces of music, and books—[all these] gain life and reality as never before. It is a great invisible sphere in which one lives and in whose reality there is no doubt. If it says in the old children's song about the angels: "Two, to cover me, two, to wake me," so is this guardianship, by good invisible powers in the morning and at night, something which grown ups need today no less than children do. Therefore you must not think that I am unhappy. What is happiness and unhappiness? It depends so little on the circumstances; it depends really only on that which happens inside a person. I am grateful every day that I have you, and that makes me happy.

We can go for weeks without experiencing this same peace of mind. Instead, we slink through our days in hopes of getting through each without conspicuous incident. At day's end, we sometimes think only to tick off our little list of grievances, not to give thanks for the honor of having one. Dietrich Bonhoeffer counted past gifts as present blessings. Even though he was about to die, his list was not an enemy's list, but a friend's and lover's list. How could Bonhoeffer experience such peace on the eve of death, whereas we find so little in the midst of life?

Bonhoeffer may well have drawn his inspiration from Saint Paul. Writing from his prison cell to the church in Philippi, Greece, Paul assures his brothers and sisters in Christ that they need not fret about his circumstances. Thanking them for their concern, Paul tells his friends not to worry. He is fine. "I have learned, in whatsoever state I am, therewith to be content. I know both how to be abased, and I know how to abound: every where and in all things I am instructed both to be full and to be hungry, both to abound and to suffer need."

These words from Paul are my favorite in all the Bible. King James Version, of course. I read the Bible for its poetry, not its accuracy, and the words "I know how to be abased and how to abound" sing in my heart. It's one of life's greatest challenges: not to get too high on our highs or fall too low with our lows. Facing death, our own or that of a loved one, keeping on an even keel may seem, even be, impossible. But it remains a worthy aspiration. If you are dying, teach your loved ones how to die. If you are "giving death," learn how to prepare for your own.

Life seems to last forever but is over in a flash. My mind these days wanders back to my childhood: playing with boats in a stream; pitching camp in a mile-high meadow and catching trout for dinner; walking from the hot-springs pool at the family ranch where I spent every summer of my youth across a frost-covered lawn without once feeling the cold. It shifts forward to my school days. How full I was of myself, so full that my father once reminded me that bumblebees are biggest when first hatched. But it was glorious. So much of my life has been glorious, when I pause to think about it. Staying up all night drinking with my friends; even though now a teetotaler, I wouldn't cash in those memories for anything in the world. Several hundred anagram scrabble games with my wife. Doing jigsaw puzzles with my kids, while keeping up with the best of their new music. And my three-book-a-week fix for as long back as I can remember. How much joy can be packed into one lifetime? I have at least a fair idea of the answer to that question.

In *Lifecraft*, I wrote that even as we choose what pictures we will hang on our walls, we can do the same with our memories. We can either call back to mind all the grim things that have befallen us and bathe in victimhood, or choose memories that make us smile. It is well not to gloss over the bad things in life, especially those we ourselves have done, because we then won't shame ourselves into doing better next time. But when it comes time to die, dust off your shiniest old memories. It will do your soul good.

They say a drowning man sees his entire life pass before his eyes. That must make drowning seem, at least, the slowest way to die. One gift a terminal illness offers us—there often being so little else we can productively do, as we lie in bed waiting to die—is the chance to see our life pass before our eyes. Each of us will choose his or her own memories to reflect on, choices made as much by temperament I suppose as by utility.

As for me, I like bright, sparkling water, not too deep, and aqua blue. So I think back on Caribbean vacations with my family on those rare occasions my father could get away from work. And I like to think back on all the books I have written, even if all of them together would probably not add up to a best seller. They are a record of my mind and heart. It gives me pleasure to have made such a record. Yet it doesn't make me proud. To one who ranks humility first among all virtues, perhaps the best thing about having a famous father is that almost nothing I accomplished would ever, in the world's eye at least, measure up. As soon as I shifted my feet from my father's ground to my own, I stopped competing with him, but I certainly never ran the danger of surpassing him. That, blessedly I think, has made all my own successes seem modest ones. Yet, I don't in the least look back on a life somehow incomplete or unrealized. Be who you are, I remind myself. I was. And I am.

My love has been far from perfect. My first wife will attest to that, and many others, I am sure, whom I have somehow disappointed along the way. To all I have hurt I here beg forgiveness, even as I freely offer my forgiveness to the handful of people who have hurt me along life's way. I don't beg shamelessly for forgiveness, but I welcome it, knowing that I can accept myself completely only if I embrace the forgiveness of others, beginning with my wife and children, whom I deeply yet imperfectly love.

That said, will my love live on forever? I believe so. And your love, too. It will certainly live on after your death, continuing to touch from heart to heart long after you have gone. We know from experience that our indifference, cynicism, and hurt feelings leave little mark. The world quickly sloughs off our complaints against it. But love it and someone, somewhere will remember. Maybe even the taxicab driver to whom you gave, for no apparent reason, an outrageously large tip. I do that more and more often these days.

I have experienced great joy writing this elegiac farewell, fighting the most convincing deadline of my life. I shall return before I go to say goodbye again to my parishioners; and, one by one, bid farewell to my friends and loved ones, when the time is right. But for now, I bid you farewell. Go forth into this fragile, blessed world we share with laughter and tears at the ready. Love, work, and serve to a fare-thee-well. And then, when your own time comes, let go. Let go for dear life.

A Closing Prayer

Christmas Eve, December 24, 2007

On this night of nights,
We have more for which to be grateful than we will ever know:
More cause to bless and cherish
And bend our knee in wonder,
More call to lift our hearts on wings of praise.

For we, too, on this very night,
Illuminated by a story and a star,
Can witness a miracle:
A birth—heralding our birth,
Pregnant with promise and oh so surpassingly strange;
A life—no less magical than ours;
A death—to charge our days with purpose,
Helping us to live in such a way
That our lives, too, will prove worth dying for.

To enter the realm of enchantment,
We must first shed our self-protective cover,
Not, as we too often and so sadly do,
Take this precious life for granted,
But unwrap the present and receive the gift,
Mysterious and charged with saving grace.

So let us, on this night of nights, set aside our shopping list of
    grievances,

Resist the nattering of our grubby little egos,
And crack our parched lives open like a seed.

Let us pray.

Let us awaken from the soul-crushing allures
Of sophisticated resignation and cynical chic,
To savor instead the world of abundance and possibility
That awaits just beyond the self-imposed limits of our
     imagination.

Let us awaken to the saving gift of forgiveness,
Where we can, in a single breath, free ourselves and free another.

Let us awaken to the possibility of love,
Body, mind, and spirit,
All-saving and all-redeeming love.

Let us awaken to the blessing of acceptance,
Expressed in a simple, saving mantra:
Want what we have; do what we can; be who we are.

Rather than let wishful thinking or regret
Displace the gratitude for all that is ours, here and now,
To savor and to save,

Let us want what we have—
Praying for health, if we are blessed with health,
For friendship, if we are blessed with friends,
For family, if we are blessed with family,
For work, if we are blessed with tasks that await our doing,
And if our lives are dark, may we remember to want nothing
     more than the loving
Affection of those whose hearts are broken by our pain.

Let us do what we can—
Not dream impossible dreams or climb every mountain,
But dream one possible dream and climb one splendid
    mountain,
That our life may be blessed with attainable meaning.

And let us be who we are—
Embrace our God-given nature and talents.
Answer the call that is ours, not another's,
Thereby enhancing our little world and the greater world we
    share.

That is my Christmas prayer,
Call it thoughtful wishing.
All we have to do is put our heart in it.
And there's one more bonus.
Unlike wishful thinking, thoughtful wishes always come true.

Amen. I love you. And may God bless us all.

Acknowledgments

All my working life, I've embraced deadlines as lifelines. A born procrastinator, I welcome ticking clocks and due dates. They get me off my duff and on to my business. For me, the business at hand was often a sermon. I've never been able to begin a sermon before Saturday morning. As for my books, the words pour out in inverse ratio to the sand remaining in my glass. When asked how I managed to write so many books, the answer is simple. I'm not a perfectionist. The perfect is the enemy of the good, someone told me once. Whether as humble proof of that little piece of wisdom or bald illustration of better living through rationalization, I've taken that adage to heart.

I began this book on Valentine's Day. It seemed a propitious time to open a book on love, but I confess that cancer was the real reason for setting my accustomed indolence aside and starting out less than a week after I had determined on a publisher. Working with the most persuasive deadline imaginable, I needed little additional incentive to get down to work.

I am delighted, for my final book, to return to the comforts of one of my favorite publishing houses, Beacon Press. *Love & Death* will be my sixth book with Beacon. The folks there have taken splendid care of me. In addition to their editorial assistance, Helene Atwan, Tom Hallock, P.J. Tierney, and Lisa Sacks guided this book through production in near-record time, for which I am grateful.

My agent, Wendy Strothman, as everyone fortunate enough

to work with her knows, is herself one of the best editors in the business. Her authors receive double service, a boon for which I am twice blessed. Throughout this period, I was also fortunate to have the companionable assistance of Justin Latterell. Justin was helping me do research for a Lincoln book that he will have to write by himself now, but he shifted gears effortlessly to aid me in this project in dozens of caring ways.

Peppered throughout this book are sermons first preached at All Souls Church and occasional passages reshaped from several of my earlier works: *Father and Son; Life Lines; Lifecraft; Bringing God Home;* and *Freedom from Fear.* I invite you to turn to them as well, should this book invite your further interest.

I cannot close without thanking my beloved children: Nathan, for your steadfastness and inner truth; Jacob, for your brilliance and radiant kindness; Nina, for your bountiful heart and gift of love; Frank, for your courage and friendship.

My cherished friends Robert Oxnam, Peter Fenn, and Jack Watson have walked with me every step of this journey, as I have tried to weave something of lasting value out of my death shroud. Robert, the first to read this volume, is more than a brother to me; Peter, my friend from childhood, has stood beside me all along life's way; and Jack, from our very first encounter, has been an ever-present joy.

Finally, my Carolyn, dear Carolyn, words will never capture my love for you. This book, in fact most everything I have accomplished over the past two decades, is for you.